# THE MARKETING STARTER

How an Entrepreneurial Spirit Will
Make You a More Savvy Marketer

## TIM HINES

# ACKNOWLEDGMENTS

My strength and tenacity to ride the wave of starter marketing throughout my career and write this book can really only be credited to God. And, the overwhelming patience and support that I needed could only have come from my amazing wife and daughter, to whom I dedicate this book.

A very special thanks to all-star marketers Beth Carr, Keith Goldberg, Rebecca Beistman, Richard Ly, Tony Weslisng, and my sister Genna Hines, who supported me by sharing their stories for the book and offering peer reviews.

A huge shout out to my sister, Lauren Fay Carlson who professionally edited this book. I could not have done it without you!

There are countless other friends and colleagues who have poured out their love and support, so many in fact I could not name them all here. Thank you all.

Finally, much love to all the great companies who employed me and took a chance when giving me my marketing starter roles. I would have never been able to write this book without all of the valuable life lessons.

# INTRODUCTION

I hope you'll indulge me with this preamble before we get to the real meat of the subject; this part will help you get a better idea of my frame of reference or lens that I use to see my marketing world. Perhaps it's better described as my worldview.

A worldview from a marketer who—for many reasons I'll divulge soon enough—has made a career of never getting anything done by becoming an expert at starting over and over.

In this book I am going to share stories of marketing upstarts from mentors, friends, colleagues, and, of course, myself. I'm hoping these insights can guide you on your marketing journey, help you make a lasting impact at your company, and give you the ability create repeatable, successful processes that will be used for years to come.

But that's up to you at the end of the day. Will you have an open mind to glean the tips that I am going to share? Will you have the drive to apply them? I am betting you will, because you picked up this book, which means you are hungry to learn how to harness the entrepreneurial spirit inside of you and work toward becoming a more savvy marketer.

When I coined the term "marketing starter," I was more than ten years deep into my career, aggressively interviewing for leadership-level marketing roles. I was running through the job hunting gauntlet, having conversation after conversation with recruiters and hiring managers at dozens of interesting companies.

I was asked the same questions repeatedly: "How would you describe your work style?" "What type of organizations do you work best in?" "What is your approach when coming into a new industry?" And I found myself answering them the same way—by alluding to my entrepreneurial spirit, thirst for autonomy, and drive to build interesting things.

Eventually, I started answering these questions by saying, "I really see myself as a marketing starter; someone who thinks like an entrepreneur, quickly learns the business, and builds new marketing programs that scale from scratch."

It was a description that resonated with my potential employers and always led to more questions and great discussion. More importantly, in the long run, it resonated deeply with me and provided me that "ah-ha!" moment when I learned how my unique skill set and perception of the business world can fit into any organization.

The newly minted tagline made me think about my experience in building marketing programs at previous organizations and gave me the foresight to understand what I desired from subsequent roles.

I have been blessed with jobs that have allowed me to use my diverse marketing experience and serve as a marketing-first entrepreneur-in-residence. In past interviews, I believe this marketing starter mentality was something my interviewers and ultimately, my new bosses, saw in me before they or I even knew what it was. I thank them for the opportunities they provided that have enabled me to share the stories in this book. It's one of those important lessons that took a long time to realize and have the clarity to scratch down on paper.

While my experience has been focused on marketing, one can most certainly be a sales starter, product starter, or even an engineer starter. Personally, I feel that a strong marketing department is the key to the success of any business, and that marketing itself requires a high level of independence and grit.

One key ingredient to creating a successful startup is marketing. What good is a wonderfully engineered product without a market to buy it? How can the product be sold without knowing who will buy it? Marketing is the hub that holds the spokes of the business together, and marketing starters are the inertia that gets the wheel spinning.

I promise this book was not written from a marketing high-horse, but as you read on about where marketing starters fit in and thrive, you'll begin to understand why I believe marketing is central to every organization. Plus, I'd be lying if I said I didn't like to toot my own horn from time to time.

During my early startup days, I had the honor of being featured in many trade publications and startup news outlets. When being interviewed, I was often asked questions like, "What is the most important thing new startup founders should consider?" or "What is the one thing you would tell founders to focus on?" My answer was always *marketing*.

Without knowing who your market is, what they want, or how to reach them, founders will be adrift. Thankfully, schooling and experience in marketing has molded me into the successful marketer that I am today.

The world is full of tenacious starters who have created earth-shattering innovations, like replacing the horse-drawn carriage with the automobile and developing the first global platform that connects friends and family with pictures and posts. We are able to start great things even if they seem small.

There will always be a better way to do something, no matter how mundane the product or process. The drive for betterment, to improve our lives, will always create opportunities for us to start.

Starter marketing is more of a perspective on operating through the organization and an implementation style of marketing tasks than a specific set of skills. Starter marketing is the mindset combined with tactics that afford marketers the ability to excel within any marketing role, especially those who are new to the role or who work within a newer organization.

Marketing starters have the attitude that marketing should provide top-tier services to the many departments it serves within its own organization. From sales managers to executives, partners to investors, the marketing department must carefully balance the needs of these internal customers while also positioning itself as an intentful expert. Marketing starters recognize this challenge and have evolved to excel.

Here's a helpful tidbit right out of the gate: Build a bond with the sales department. After all, as simplistic as this may sound, without sales driving revenue, there can be no marketing, and without marketing driving leads for sales, there will be no revenue. And around and around we go.

Marketing (and the starter-minded people who live it every day) is the catalyst that helps get the organization going and is deeply entwined with nearly every other function within the business, from sales to product development to human resources.

Marketing is much more than churning out one-sheets and blog posts—it is a core methodology that a company should believe in and support (something you should ask interviewers). For the most part, marketing works in the shadows while other teams get all the glory.

Marketing starters are fine with this; their thrill comes from the success they help to create. They get the concept of passing the baton to let others finish the race, but also understand the importance of running the first part of the race as fast as they can.

Whether you are employed by a company or you are a startup founder, having a marketing starter mentality—or hiring someone who does—is crucial to building successful marketing programs. Certainly, the right people with the right skillset get the job done, but having your own starter mentality gives you a backbone of autonomy, growth, and grit.

Once you approach your career from the perspective of a marketing starter, there comes a sense of urgency, excitement, and agency that allows you to more boldly command the attention of company leadership. You'll more easily be able to garner the resources required to make such initiatives happen the way you envision them.

Throughout this book, I'll be sharing stories and tips to help mold you as a marketing starter. Some of them may be ridiculously obvious while others you may have never tried. Keeping all of that in mind, I tried not to go too far down the rabbit hole with any one of the ideas, so as to keep things conceptual and leave the tactical application to you.

I am challenging you to really think about how the upcoming tips and anecdotes apply to your unique situation and how you might weave them into your next steps as a professional.

So, what do you say… shall we get started?

# CHAPTER 1

## ARE YOU A MARKETING STARTER?

The way to get started is to quit talking and begin doing.

–Walt Disney

M arketing may be one of the most diversified career sectors in business today. Off the top of my head I can name product marketing, brand management, advertising, content marketing, field marketing, public relations, marketing operations, partnership marketing, and email marketing.

Need I go on?

There are a million specialties that any eager marketer can focus on in his or her career, but nowhere on a job board will you see the title *marketing starter*.

Go ahead, type "marketing starter" into a Google Jobs search and see what comes back. A whole lot of nothing. That's because "marketing starter" isn't a job title or specific type of marketing; it's a unique style or mindset that can—and, dare I say, should—be applied to any marketing role.

Many soon-to-be marketers are coached by college guidance counselors to pick a specific aspect of marketing on which to focus their careers because they believe that high-specialization is the way to be the most successful. While these would-be wise coaches are partially right, I believe that having a wide skill set with the ability to focus on high-specialization as needed is the way to go. This wide background gives marketers the unique ability to fit into many different roles where they can be starters and lead teams.

Starter marketing isn't a marketing specialization; it's a mindset that compiles a little bit of know-how from all the marketing career tracks into one wonderful approach that can get any marketing program off the ground. A marketing starter needs to know just enough from each key form of marketing to build successful marketing programs and manage intelligent teams with the right amount of humility to lean on their internal experts to champion their individual initiatives. Knowing these essential building blocks helps a marketing starter understand the marketing process and empathize with their counterparts.

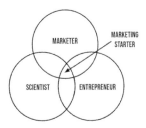

Who are these marketing starters? A marketing starter is one part broad marketer, one part entrepreneur, and one part scientist, all bundled up in a blanket of hustle. Marketing starters are able to combine a marketing generalist background with an entrepreneurial attitude, giving them the unique ability to juggle a multitude of marketing tasks. Think of a marketing starter as a jack-of-all-trades or a marketing handyman, someone who enters any marketing mess and makes the fixes necessary to make any company's marketing machine run smoothly.

Marketing starters are also builders, the constructors of grand marketing schemes, and can also design and engineer the processes that get marketing plans off the ground. They draft the blueprints, document the protocols, and recruit the team. They have a can-do attitude to build and lead their marketing departments.

Imagine an energetic and innovative growth hacker, someone

responsible for driving growth for a company using whatever tools and channels are available to them. Growth hacking was a popular term around 2014–2015, especially in the startup scene where small, high-energy companies needed growth marketing experts to come in and help scale rapidly. The enlightened mind of a creative growth hacker is the perfect persona for my first model of a marketing starter.

> **TIP 1:**
> Imagine your favorite marketing track (perhaps you're in it now) and ask yourself what you enjoy most about it. Think about what you would do if your boss asked you to scrap your current job description and rewrite the script of your role from scratch. Are you up to the task? This is a good thought experiment to see if you're a marketing starter.

I am most definitely a marketing starter. Throughout my career, all of my marketing roles have involved starter marketing in some form. From developing value-added channels to building a corporate marketing department from scratch to crafting launch plans for startups—my roles have been hyper-focused on either building first-time marketing initiatives or starting something new in marketing for the first time. I am able to do this because of my entrepreneurial spirit mixed with my marketing generalist background.

One way to figure out if you're a marketing starter is to take my sure-fire marketing starter quiz. There's nothing super scientific about it really, but the questions will help you figure out if you fit the very uniquely-shaped mold. Think about them and answer honestly to yourself.

1. Do you enjoy building new things from the ground up?

Marketing starters need to be comfortable with building things from scratch.

2. Do you thrive in small to mid-sized companies or in brand new roles? More often than not, starter roles will exist in small to mid-sized companies, but I'd be remiss to completely forget the progressive, larger enterprise that brings in a starter or two to mix things up.

3. Are you well organized and comfortable being part of a smaller team responsible for many marketing tasks? Being a starter requires next-level organization because no one is going to do it for you.

4. Are you okay with doing all the work and receiving little recognition? We will discuss this at length in a later chapter, but starters need to be okay not getting constant pats on the back. It's most certainly a grind and a long road ahead before recognition will be attained.

5. Do you embrace volatility and stay flexible in your plans? As humans, this goes against our very nature. We quest for stability and patterns, but marketing starters need to be okay with shedding their nature to pursue their goals

If you honestly answered YES to all the questions in this mini quiz, then you are certainly on the way to the marketing starter mentality, or at least get the concept. If you answered NO to some or all of the questions, don't fret. By the end of the book, once I have shared stories and explained some of these concepts further, you might shift into the starter realm, which will transform your career into one that challenges the status quo.

**The Ideal Marketing Starter**

I have read article after article about the best pathways to follow in marketing careers. Some say hyper-specialization is the right path while others say generalization is the way to go. At the end of the day, it all comes down to the kind of organization you ultimately see yourself joining. Typically, larger organizations employ more specialized marketers and smaller organizations look for people who offer more of a broad stroke.

It is well understood that no channel of marketing can stand on its own; content needs a website, social media needs content, and the website needs advertising. This is precisely why, at smaller organizations in which the marketer must wear many hats, marketing starters are in high demand.

I have worked for only a few large companies in my career, and I must admit that my starter skills were far less appreciated there. The generalist framework that I apply to my methods has allowed my marketing starter mentality to flourish. I am what many people in the business call a "T-shaped marketer."

Not familiar with the concept? For a quick crash course, the T represents the shape of the marketer's knowledge and skills. The breadth of various skills are represented horizontally and the specialization vertically. Basically, a T-shaped marketer combines the wide breadth of knowledge of a generalist, who has familiarity with various competencies and no major depth in one particular skill, with the deep skills of a specialist (I-shaped marketer) who has competencies and expertise beholden within their specialty. Another way to describe T-shaped marketers would be "specialized generalists" which follow my equation above, $I + G = T$. I for specialist, G for generalist, and T for specialized generalist.

DISCIPLINE COMPETENCY

| SEO | Social Media | Content | Communications | Analytics |
|-----|--------------|---------|----------------|-----------|
| | Manage Engage Contests | Blogs Studies Papers | Email Press Conferences | |

DEPTH OF EXPERTISE

T-shaped marketers have become a Swiss army knife with the ability to take on a variety of marketing challenges, which makes them attractive to employers, especially startups who need someone with a wide skill set that fits the needs of the company. I would strongly argue that T's are the most open-minded and have the ability to adapt their marketing skills to any situation. T's can also quickly ramp up their abilities in specializations, making them perfect marketing starters.

Jess McMullin of Situ Strategy once said, "There's a seduction to being an expert, an assumption in society that credibility relies on deep (and narrow) expertise. However, for people operating at the edges, intersections, and overlaps where innovation thrives, being a generalist is far more powerful." I would build on Jess's thought by saying that being a generalist with a deep well of expertise makes you a much more effective marketer.

> **TIP 2:**
> Create your own skills competency chart and see how you pan out. Be honest about your knowledge and skills to assess where you can grow and shape yourself into more of a T-shaped marketer.

You might be asking, "Can I still have a marketing starter mentality and be an I-shaped or a G-shaped marketer? Of course, you can!

These shapes and models are more about the skills depth and knowledge breadth than an attitude or mindset. You can apply marketing starter tactics to any marketing role at any size company with any skill set. Whether you're a growth marketer, product marketer, or content marketer, starter marketing is a way of positioning yourself with the ability to build new things.

It is also a great way for generalists to stand out in the new, hyper-specialist world and for specialists to extend the olive branch across marketing specialties. That being said, a T-shaped marketer does have an advantage when entering a role that requires a marketing starter approach. I would recommend researching how you can become a strong T-shaped marketer to allow yourself to be moldable into a variety of marketing roles and companies.

**From Humble Beginnings**

My marketing journey started at an internship while I was in school at the University of Illinois. My senior year strategic marketing and advertising class was assigned a semester-long advertising program that we, as an entire class, had to plan and coordinate together. The class served as an ad agency for a big name client and was broken up into about five teams focused on different components of the semester-long campaign. We built a multi-channel, interactive advertising campaign across the university campus including events, traditional advertising, text message campaigns, and on-site promotions.

Are you wondering who the client was? Well, if I told you I would have to kill you, because it was the CIA and they swore me to secrecy. Oops…. Now that you know, the goal of the campaign was to drive awareness of CIA careers on the college campus.

The CIA loved our results and applied many of our tactics to their national ad campaign that was planned for launch later in the year. A few of us, including yours truly, were offered positions in the CIA marketing department in Virginia. It was an honor, but I wanted to pursue opportunities in my home city of Chicago. Also, going through basic training for a desk job just wasn't my speed.

My very first full-time marketing role came shortly after college graduation. I served as the email marketing coordinator for Tickets-Now, which is now Ticket Exchange by Ticketmaster. They were a leading secondary event ticketing marketplace, and email was an enormous revenue channel for the company—so large that the email channel that I developed drew in over $2 million in gross revenue.

The gig itself was a simple one: manage customer subscriptions, update email content, send calculated campaigns, and partner with the design team to keep the emails looking fresh.

One of the most interesting, or annoying nuances to the job, depending on how you look at it, was preparing a variety of emails with different ticket inventory numbers without knowing which one to send until late at night when West Coast baseball playoff games would finish up (I was based in Chicago at the time).

This was long before MLB and ESPN apps existed to send alerts with game scores. I'd have to stay up late most nights either watching the game or hitting refresh on baseball websites hoping the nine innings would not turn into ten, eleven, or twelve. In those wee hours of the Central Time Zone, I had to be careful as I sent out the correct staged email once the game concluded. Luckily, I was able to come to the office later those days to make up for my 2 a.m. bedtimes.

I did quite a bit of other marketing gigs after TicketsNow, but let's skip ahead a little bit to when I first dipped my toe into the entrepreneurial realm.

## My First Startup

My first startup project role came after being laid off from my marketing analyst position at Tribune Media Group. After nearly five years with the company, this layoff gave way for me to venture out on my own and develop my first startup, BTSocial, short for Business Traveler Social.

I love business travel, so I created a news and networking resource for travelers that combined events with a social platform. However, just because I had a passion for business travel didn't mean I had any expertise in the market. So, learning the ways of the mighty corporate travel industry was an immediate priority. This was where I learned my first marketing starter hacks.

Working on BTSocial, I learned how important marketing is in building an idea from scratch. During that time, I was interviewed multiple times by small media outlets that asked me what was most important for new startup founders to learn.

Time and time again, I answered, "Marketing." I would explain that knowing the size of your market, the behaviors of the market, and how to reach out to said market were crucial to any new startup. I also believe it's important that companies have a basic marketing plan that includes a clear understanding of market trends and demands before they launch an event or create a business plan. Without this, new founders will be lost.

I got to practice wearing a lot of hats in that early startup endeavor; CMO was only one of them. I was also CEO, COO, CPO, and even CFO during tax season and explaining financial models to potential investors. When I was wearing my marketing hat, I spent hours upon hours researching the best ways to reach our market—both travel companies and travelers.

I had to answer tough questions like, "Where do these groups spend their time online?", "How can I reach them en masse?", "What ultimately is going to drive them to social tools and events?", and "What strategic partnerships will help us grow?" Honestly, the list was endless. The biggest value I got from starting that company was laying the groundwork for what would ultimately make up my marketing starter mentality.

## Chief Marketing Ninja

How I learned to answer those nagging marketing questions helped me immensely when launching my second startup, CurbNinja. The app—which is still live today and combines my passion for motorcycles with my inner cartography geek—helps urban motorcyclists find the safest and most reliable places to park in congested urban centers. I always described it as Waze for motorbike parking.

Like with BTSocial, I had to wear every hat, which enabled me to get much, much better at the marketing side of the business. I leveraged social media, content, press, and events to get the word out about the app. I posted videos on our YouTube channel and packed our Instagram feed with awesome pictures. However, what ultimately kept our growth steady was word of mouth. We relied on and grew because of the tightly-knit community of motorcyclists around the world who shared the app with each other to make their commutes and urban exploration a little easier.

The marketing starter approach with CurbNinja was to keep things simple. Simple name, simple branding, simple solution, simple marketing plan. And it worked. The over-complication of BTSocial, and not having a clean, easy-to-explain solution, taught me to craft a streamlined approach for CurbNinja.

During the startup trials I had absolutely no clue what I was doing—but at least I was well aware of my cluelessness. I sought help from mentors, colleagues, friends, and even enrolled in startup education programs. My passion to own my work and be a champion in marketing coalesced into my professional positioning later in my career. This positioning had to be tested and challenged—and that all began when I found myself in my first intrapreneur marketer role (a.k.a. marketing starter role).

**From the Inside Out**

My first in-house marketing starter role came when I followed the siren song of the West Coast and moved from Chicago to San Francisco. I started at Vendini (now part of AudienceView) three days after I had packed as many of my belongings as I could into four duffel bags and dropped them in my rental room in Berkeley. A few months later I went back to Chicago to get the rest of my stuff and my Old English Bulldog, Santo, and drove across the country in a 1995 Dodge Ram pickup that I bought for $1,500 and later sold for $1,500 to reduce my moving expenses. But that's a story for a later time….

Initially, I had applied for a product marketing manager role with Vendini, but after a few interviews, the CMO (my soon-to-be manager) saw the spark of a marketing starter in me (before I even recognized this myself) and decided to create a new role just for me.

He saw the combination of my marketing background and startup experience as a way for him to fill this role designed to build new marketing channels and help fortify their current Software as a Service (SaaS) offering. The role was channel marketing (development) manager with the primary task of building Vendini's consumer-facing channels that would help create more value for their existing B2B solutions.

Vendini was a B2B SaaS ticketing platform and, until the time I arrived, it provided solely a backend solution to their 3,000+ customers across the country, such as performing arts centers, comedy clubs, college sports venues, and more. Where they were struggling to compete was on the B2C front—they lacked a viable channel for promoting their customers' events. They found they would lose deals to other ticketing companies who had consumer portals that served as marketing channels for their customers, like Eventbrite. So, my role was to create and promote new B2B2C marketing channels, thus serving as an intrapreneur. In a sense, I was building a business within a business.

My boss, the CMO, often referred to my methods as "duct tape and chicken wire," which was a perfect analogy. I had to wrangle engineers and product managers to build what I needed. I had to lean on the marketing team to help with design work. I had to train the customer success team on my new product's capabilities. I had to ensure that the sales team was properly communicating the value of my work. All of this while leading a small team of marketing starters that managed all of the consumer channels under our belts.

If that's not starter marketing, then I don't know what is! Unfortunately, as I will soon come to understand is a theme in my career, I was laid off from the company along with many other counterparts. We all had to start again.

## Second-Time Starter

After Vendini, I was the director of marketing at a mid-sized digital advertising agency. I was tasked with building a marketing department from scratch, complete with the tools, personnel, protocols, and plans to get the job done. My team and I did every marketing task under the sun. It was a solid B2B role in which the department's north star was driving marketing qualified leads and satisfying sales' unquenchable thirst for leads.

Like at Vendini, this was the ideal marketing starter role. I was able to make an immediate impact and drive tangible results by fixing broken marketing processes and laying the groundwork for programs that are in use today.

Within the first six months, the COO charged my team with the tasks of rolling out Salesforce company-wide (and training everyone), implementing a new marketing automation tool, and building a new corporate website. All of this was to be done on the heels of performing a brand refresh with all the fixins, including global messaging and positioning.

It was a tall order, especially since there were only three of us and we also had our regular day-to-day marketing functions to do. Luckily, my team was made up of hustlers who were receptive to the ways of the marketing starter. I was able to show them the excitement behind the build with the promise of gaining expertise to mold them to be stronger T-shaped marketers.

## Third Time's the Charm

My next starter role was with Dialpad, a cloud-based telephony software company, also known as universal communications as a service (UCaaS). Indeed, a mouthful!

The company was growing like gangbusters and their marketing specialty needs were increasing, especially around partnerships. I was brought in to serve as director of global partner marketing, which was a brand new role under a newly organized marketing team led by the VP of corporate marketing.

She was so new, in fact, that I was her first hire since coming on board. She was in place for just three weeks before I started, which proved to be a great way to build this new marketing channel together.

I was responsible for supporting the rapidly growing channel side of the business. At first, I was the channel manager's sole supporter, taking over from the strained corporate marketing team. Later, I expanded my team to better accommodate the channel manager's needs.

I don't think I had ever felt so needed in a marketing starter role before this. The underserved channel team was in great need of dedicated marketing support and systems to help them grow.

This role was a true builder role, one that required all processes to be developed from scratch. What made this role interesting was the ability to build something new inside a well-established company offering the security and ability to learn from a greater marketing department.

Unfortunately, also like Vendini, my time at Dialpad was cut short by yet another layoff—the fifth of my career. Once again I had to dust myself off and start again. I have some tips later on to help you keep an eye out for layoff potential.

## One Final Case Study

When I served as Head of Marketing at Rockbot, I was the head honcho when it came to all things marketing.

The company was small (around 30 people at the time), and super agile, but desperately needed a marketing leader to take charge, clean house, and ramp up marketing efforts. I came in to fill the shoes of a seasoned and capable marketer who certainly had the chops to build and manage a successful marketing program but who lacked the agility and flexibility of a marketing starter..

The previous marketing leader came with the education and

accolades that looked amazing on paper but did not translate well within Rockbot's startup environment. He was more prescriptive in his methods, which let him flex his attention to detail and delegate workload. However, it also left him rigid, not having the flexibility needed to work cross-functionally within a smaller startup culture. This was something the team echoed emphatically when I came aboard. They never doubted his abilities, but they ultimately saw he was more like a big corporate type who was more reliant on processes than the scrappy approach needed within a lean startup organization. Thankfully, that's where I thrive, and was brought on board to roll up my sleeves and get shit done.

As you can see, my experience has been vast, but the most enjoyable and impactful roles have been those in which I got to be a marketing starter. From startups to growth companies to enterprise and anywhere in between, I have always strived to be a starter in some form.

There is always some new ground to break or a new trail to forge, no matter the role. The bottom line for marketing starters is to focus your marketing skills on building something new, or fixing something broken..

Whether working for or building a startup or joining a mid-size or large organization, there is a place for a marketing starter. It all comes down to the project, and if that project allows you to exercise one of your finely-tuned marketing skills.

Something to always remember is that the marketing starter road can be treacherous, volatile, and lonely at times, but the payoff is great. You get to be the designer, the maker, the implementer all in one—what other career path can offer you that?

## Greetings from Marketing Island

Pack your bags and get to the airport to feed your starter wanderlust —you're headed to Marketing Island.

Imagine for a second that you wake up from an unconscious state with the sun shining in your face, the sound of waves crashing in the not-so-distant background. Not to forget the uncomfortable feeling of sand down your crack. You stand erect and realize you're on a deserted island and no one is around.

Just imagine the movie *Castaway,* starring Tom Hanks. Yep, now you got it!

Now that we have the picture of you on a deserted island somewhere in the tropical Pacific, I can make the point that when we venture out as marketing starters and first enter a new office, we often feel like we're waking up on a deserted marking island and have to figure everything out for ourselves.

In the previous section, I gave you some case studies of my marketing starter roles and how I was often left to my own devices to figure things out and make my programs work. I often felt like I was dropped on an island all by myself, with limited tools and resources, and was told to build a boat by hand or engineer a makeshift bridge to connect my island to the mainland (and with civilization).

Since marketing starters are industrious and adventurous, this challenge might sound alluring. Of course, you're never without some sort of resources. Remember my time with Vendini, where I had to build my programs with "duct tape and chicken wire," as the CMO so eloquently put it? I was certainly on Marketing Island then, with limited resources at my disposal to build my programs from the ground—or should I say sand—up. But I got it done.

I'm totally cool with being stuck on Marketing Island. In fact, I enjoy it. I have made a career out of parachuting from one lonesome Marketing Island to another and building bridges between them.

You can do the same, though not every island or scenario is the same. Some islands might be bigger and more difficult to navigate. Others might have more resources for you to use to build your bridge. No matter the island you might find yourself on, it's important to get a good map of what you're jumping into before you do it. Your experience and fortitude will determine which island challenge you can handle and which you can't.

TIP 3:

During your interview process, or when exploring a prospective role change, get an idea of what your Marketing Island looks like and what resources you'll have before you jump out of the plane.

I've read a lot of articles and sat through many webinars about how to be a marketing team of one or manage a very small team. Go ahead and Google "marketing team of one" and see what pops up. Blog articles, videos, listicles—they all have great tips on how to be a successful lone ranger marketer.

You'll see headlines such as, "Create a reusable marketing strategy," "Build your automation framework," and "Stay current on marketing trends." These and many more fantastic tips are available, but no matter how many tips you ingest, there will always be a certain amount of pioneering you'll have to do on your own.

No Marketing Island is the same. Just remember to pack some sunscreen.

**The Starter to Be**

Are you starting to get the concept of a marketing starter yet? You should now have the knowledge to determine if you are one, and if you are, fantastic! The rest of this book will help you hone your skills and add new tactics to your repertoire.

If you don't believe you're quite there yet, that's okay, too. Chapter two is where we'll get started training you to apply this mentality to any marketing role you may be in today or will find yourself in the future. It all boils down to the idea that marketers must have a worldview of making change within their organizations and their careers.

The very first thing you need to do is to keep an open mind and, no matter how difficult it may seem, think like an entrepreneur. If you treat your marketing tasks like they are helping your own business get off the ground, half your battle to marketing starter stardom has already been won.

So what if you're not a marketing starter today? Anyone can become one with enough focus and grit. I would not have considered myself a marketing stater when I took my first role as email marketing coordinator at TicketsNow.

I was focused, learning the ins and outs of email marketing and trying my best to keep my head above water in that post-college super junior role. Nevertheless, even a job I was scrambling to learn helped shape me into a marketing starter—and so can yours! We just need to reorient your mind and flip your perspective so you can apply the starter mentality to all that you do.

So what do you say? Should we get started starting?

# CHAPTER 2

## LEARN THE BUSINESS

Play by the rules, but be ferocious.

–Phil Knight
Co-founder, Nike

L et me introduce you to Katie, a young marketer in her second role, who is one week into her new job as a content marketing specialist at a mid-sized digital advertising agency.

Despite Katie still being green, she has worked for a hyper-growth company in the past and has an inkling for what it takes to be a marketing starter. She has come to her new company with tenacity and willingness to learn and make change.

Her boss, the director of marketing, is also a keen marketing starter and has empowered Katie to take on the challenges of her new role.

Katie digs in.

While she has been set up with training slots with the executives, as well as product, sales, and operations teams, she knows that what she needs is to increase her domain expertise of the business.

So she takes it upon herself to start learning as much as she can about the nuances of the business, its competitors, and the industry itself. She registers for webinars, sets up calls with customers, and sits in on sales pitches. She knows that her tenacity and marketing chops will push her to learn what she lacks in the digital advertising space.

Katie also buys books on Amazon and schedules regular meetings with the CEO to learn the ways of the business. She does all of this to better understand what it takes to be part of a fast-moving marketing team.

Katie's starter mentality has positioned her to be a special kind of marketer, one who applies her skills to create blockbuster campaigns and knows the business like the back of her hand.

We should all take a lesson from Katie's marketing starter approach and be relentless in learning the ins and outs of our new roles, companies, and industries. Whether you are working for a B2B or B2C company, you should be confident in your marketing expertise and find ways to make your formulas work for any company in any industry. What needs to be learned, however, are the nuances of the business. It's imperative to have a solid grasp on these details before you can start to market properly.

In this chapter, I'll share some starter approaches to learn the business, which any successful marketer must do in order to market said business. Katie gets it—she has the awareness to know that she is still fresh in her marketing career and to this particular role, leaving a big gap to fill with learning. Like Katie, we all need to be aware of where we are in our knowledge, and we should never forget that we will never stop learning the businesses.

## It All Begins with Why

If you haven't read Simon Sinek's book *Start With Why* or watched his TED Talk, I strongly encourage you to take 20 minutes to do so, especially for the sake of reading this section. I'm going to reference it quite a bit. It's easy to find on YouTube, but make sure to watch the full-length version.

Go ahead, set down the book and watch. I'll wait....

And we're back.

While Simon's *Golden Circle* philosophy transcends all facets of business and leadership, I truly feel why-based thinking is especially pivotal when applied to marketing. Why is a mission-driven way of thinking that should flow through the organization like red blood cells through the body. The company's why is the lifeblood that keeps employees engaged, products innovative, and customers returning and advocating.

In his talk, Simon stated, "People don't buy what you do, they buy why you do it." This couldn't be more true. If your company has a clear why, employees who share the same belief will want to work there and stay longer and customers will be more loyal and spend more money. Simon also said it's not your goal to do business with everyone, rather only with those who believe what you believe. This is something you can take to heart as you build your marketing campaigns and messaging.

The fact of the matter is the entities that have a clear why are more aware of themselves and their business, and easier to market. So your marketing department should be extremely focused on why —why the company exists, why they make what they make, why they serve a specific client base, why they are in their industry, etc.

What business are you in? Is ADT in the alarm business or the feeling safe business? Does Ford make cars or do they provide mobility for anyone? Does Salesforce make CRM software or are they in the sales efficiency business? To get a real understanding of a company's why, you have to look past the features of what they make and focus on the human benefit. That human benefit will point you in the right direction of understanding the company's why.

And here's a hint: The answer to these questions should never be "to make money." I believe that if money is the principal motivation of a company's existence, then it—and your marketing plans—are doomed.

Before you can start building your marketing campaigns, it's important to know your company's why. Being a student of the Sinek school, I take it upon myself to discover the company's why immediately after getting my new desk organized and email operational.

At the leadership level, understanding this right away is imperative to helping you get organized and build or run your team. Your marketing plans and programs need to reflect the goals of the company, goals which are driven by the mission. You'll also want to establish a clear why for your team, no matter how small.

Even if you're not in a marketing leadership role, having a clear understanding of the company's why is uber important. I would suggest putting light pressure on your manager to clearly explain the company's why and mission and how it translates into your marketing team's tasks and approach. It's both the responsibility of your manager and you as an employee to have an unadulterated understanding of the mission and share the same belief to maintain a cohesive team.

> **TIP 4:**
> Ask your manager if they know the company's why. If they know, then ask how they apply that thinking to your team's duties. If they don't, then you should add this to your list of items to discover.

Unearthing your new employer's why might prove to be a challenge, especially if you are coming into a long-standing organization that has not clearly communicated its why since the beginning of time. Startup founders actually have a great advantage here; they are able to clearly state why they decided to launch their businesses in the first place. They typically are brimming with passion and can talk to you all day long about their mission and vision.

Throughout my career, I've heard people question why anyone would want to work for a startup, since it usually comes with high volatility, long hours, and often below-market pay. The answer is that the startup is really good at conveying their why and sharing their beliefs, which also makes doing their marketing a lot of fun. That startup culture runs deep and creates a real sense of belonging.

For more tenured organizations, however, the definition of why might be a little muddier. So grab some boots and a shovel—we're going digging to rediscover the company's why.

The best source of why should be your company's CEO or founding team. Hopefully, you work for an organization that allows for easy-enough access to the company's leader of culture. During meetings with the CEO, I have always asked questions to help them convey why they went into business in the first place and what they believe in. Other executives within the company should also be able to clearly articulate the company's why, as well as the overall direction and goals.

If your company is a little more vertical, you may need to get more creative to connect with your CEO and executive team.

Don't be shy—marketing starters never should be!

> **TIP 5:**
> Create a company-wide survey asking if your counterparts know the organization's why.
> Analyze the results to see how well aligned the organization is around the company's mission.

Beyond the executive team, it's helpful to interact with other managers and employees across departments to see how well the company's mission resonates with them, and whether or not they buy into it. If they don't, it is unlikely that customers will, which makes your job as a marketer very difficult. By the end of this discovery mission, you should have a good grasp on why the company exists and why customers want to do business with it. If not, then you can help coach the company into clearly defining its why and getting company-wide buy-in.

This is far beyond a marketer's job description, but you're a marketing starter, remember? So I'm sure you're up for it. Good luck!

## Take Time to Get Plugged In

One of the first things I do to learn the business when sitting at my new desk is to start researching industry news outlets, events, and experts where I snag articles and sound bites to sharpen my industry acumen. I'll subscribe to industry newsletters and RSS feeds from news sites and follow as many key industry influencers on social media as I can find, sticking to LinkedIn and Twitter. I also join industry-related professional groups on LinkedIn and try to engage as much as possible.

These groups also create a great canvas for you to share content you create. Asking your counterparts what sites they frequent, what newsletters they read, and what professional groups they joined on LinkedIn is also a good way to source different places to share content. I have always found that CEOs have a great list of industry information sources.

It also never hurts to put your business shirt on and get activated with professional groups in-person, like industry association events and meetings. Never underestimate the power of networking!

> **TIP 6:**
> Create daily Google Alerts for your company's name, your CEO, your industry, your customers, and key industry influencers to keep tabs on what's happening in your world.

Believe it or not, some industry publications still print magazines and bulletins. I know what you're thinking… subscribe to printed literature? YES!

This may be best for you overachievers, but some publications will actually print unique or more in-depth content than what's available online. Sign up for them and have them mailed to your office. When they arrive, give them a good skim for content that might be worth a full read and fold them into your weekly reading research.

Another fantastic avenue that helps you get plugged in is to follow your new company's online presence and read, read, read. Of course, you already did this during your interview process and in preparation for your first day, since you're such a savvy interviewer and soon-to-be employee. But on the off chance that you didn't do this already or that you stopped once you found your new desk, you should find your company's social media pages, blog, and press releases, and read up.

This is especially important for marketing roles because you should familiarize yourself with the brand voice and how the company positions itself to the outside world. I've worked for companies that had a weekly internal newsletter that showcased what was happening in each department within the company but also highlighted news articles and industry insights. They already did half the work for me and served it up on a silver platter. All I had to do now was make time to read.

It can be difficult in your first month or so at a new gig to make time between training, meetings, and actual work, but slotting time to check out what your company is putting out into the ether will make you a better marketer. And if it will intersect with your job in any way, like if you're on the social media team or PR team, it should come as second nature.

**Sales Will Show You the Way**

As I mentioned in the introduction, I firmly believe that marketing's relationship with sales is the most important to the company, as one cannot live without the other. Taking an interest in sales team activities and understanding how to support them should be paramount to learning the business.

Marketing should participate in recurring sales meetings—weekly, monthly, or quarterly—and come prepared with updates on initiatives that directly influence the sales team. Marketing may also have projects that impact fundraising, recruiting, and other major business initiatives. Whatever constituent you help, get to their damn meeting.

Ask the meeting leader, typically the sales executive, to create a bullet point in the agenda for marketing to provide its update. A representative from marketing should always have a seat at the table in sales meetings. It may not need to be the marketing leader every time, but someone should be present to show sales that you've got their back. It's actually great exposure for junior marketing reps to join the meeting, both to learn the business and to sharpen their presentation and communication skills.

> **TIP 7:**
> If you are in a marketing leadership role, attempt
> to become best friends with the sales leaders.
> Set up recurring meetings to help them
> advocate for marketing and vice versa.

On the road, salespeople love to schmooze with prospects and customers. I love to tag along with sales reps to client meetings or hosted events. Not only do I get a chance to break up my normal work cadence, but it proves to be an almost imperative way to learn the business.

I'll approach a rep talking with a prospective customer and watch them work their magic. Seeing reps talk about the business and answer questions firsthand is greater than any other customer research you can do as a new-to-the-business marketer. A lot of times you see this happen en masse at large industry events like conferences.

Conferences are a ton of fun and a great learning experience for marketing starters to see the sales team in action and learn from other experts in attendance. This is where marketing starters need to overcome their shyness (if they had any to begin with). Tagging along with sales in any of these scenarios is one of the best ways to learn the business and the industry and build your relationship with the sales team.

Venturing off on your own to schmooze with people in the industry at these shows will pay you back in droves. Come prepared with a list of questions you want to have answered. Jot them down or memorize them, and as you chat up a fellow marketer over your mass-produced salad and chicken dishes for lunch, ask away.

Take notes on a pad or in your phone right after, then compile them with your other session notes. Following the event, review and recall the conversations to see how well your questions were answered.

These shows can often feel like drinking from a fire hose, especially if you're new to the industry, but the exposure you'll get is priceless. Plus, at conferences, you can help man the booth, making sure it's up to marketing's standards and using the valuable facetime to test messaging. What better way to test your company's new brand message than by doing it 100 times over a couple days on your feet.

## What Other Departments Have to Say

Learning from colleagues doesn't have to stop with attending conferences with your sales folks. Another great way to get plugged in to learning the business is to sit in on other department meetings to learn their struggles and lingo.

These meetings may be completely unrelated to anything you are working on in marketing, so asking to sit in may seem a little out of left field. But trust me, you will learn a ton and, more often than not, the group will appreciate you taking an interest in what they do at the company, especially if you're serving in a leadership role.

In my first director role, I spent a lot of time mingling with other departments, especially on my mission to unearth the company's why. It was an enlightening project to marry the two widely different perspectives of the executives and the customer-centric reps in the trenches. I also made time to sit in on department meetings where I could get updates on other departments and share anything from marketing that might affect them.

> **TIP 8:**
> Schedule interviews with customer-focused representatives to get their perspective on the business. They have great intel on the customers' inner-most desires.

You should also make time to meet with other directors and key managers who take responsibility for the company's direction. Especially take time to sit down with those who have the most tenure, as they are the most likely to share their unfiltered and candid opinions about the company and pass along their accumulated wisdom.

When I first came into my role at Dialpad, I spent the first two weeks connecting with all the key stakeholders who would be interacting with me. First, I scheduled meetings with everyone on my team whom I would support, then other leaders from sales, marketing, and customer success. It was important for me to understand their intersections with my new role and how we might work best together from their perspective.

Lastly, although they're often very busy, attempt to schedule learning sessions with the CEO or founder if you can. These can be more frequent at first but can be spread out eventually to once a quarter.

These meetings help marketing starters two-fold: First, they will help you get a good grasp of the overall vision of the company, which will help you when building direction for your department. Ask a ton of questions and get your leaders to share their ideas about what they want to see coming out of marketing. This will help you to better learn and manage expectations so that your plans properly reflect them and that your deliverables are clear.

Second, these check-ins will give your work much-needed exposure at the highest levels of the company. It's never good to have the executives wondering what is happening on the marketing front, especially in the early days while you are building your programs. Seize this opportunity to share your plans and tout what work has already been completed.

With all of these meeting opportunities, your calendar can get pretty jam-packed, so consider moments outside office hours. Invite your counterparts to mid-morning coffee, lunch, or for a quick happy hour to build relationships and discuss how you can work better together. Oh, and always offer to pick up the tab!

**The Customer Knows Best**

Who would have ever thought that talking to customers would be like unlocking a Pandora's box of your business information? Well, hopefully *you* did, because everything your business does at the end of the day is designed to please the customer and ultimately make them open their wallets.

Your job as a marketer is to contribute to an overall plan of attracting new customers, keeping current customers happy, and increasing their lifetime value—also known as getting them to spend more money when they do buy.

Customers may have a little or a lot to say about your business, but no matter what they say, what you'll hear will be extremely valuable. There's a reason most mid-size and enterprise companies have a customer marketing team dedicated to learning about the customer's experience and sharing that publicly through testimonials or case studies.

Perhaps you are in this role today and are responsible for sending out the annual or bi-annual customer survey. Or maybe you're working on a new referral program that handsomely rewards customers for bringing in new business. Either way, those functions can teach us an awful lot about our business.

Surveys can obviously offer the most clarity, depending on the questions that are asked. Questions such as, "How would you rate our onboarding experience?," "How satisfied are you with our service?," and "What can we do to improve our renewal process?" are great questions to shed light on what the company is doing right or wrong. But what about the answers you don't get or the referrals that don't happen?

Most of your customers will stay silent when being surveyed or asked to engage in public testimonials or referrals, which makes customer marketing difficult. However, there is an opportunity to learn a lot about your business from customers, no matter where it comes from.

I mentioned earlier that a great way to learn the business is to sit in on sales calls and listen to how the sales team positions the business and responds to questions. Well, the exact same practice goes for your customer service team.

Their customer-facing calls can offer a great wealth of information as they navigate the treacherous waters of customer service. There's nothing more honest than a customer scorned. You can learn a ton by understanding the needs and desires of your customers, and this can be achieved by hearing from them directly on customer service calls.

If you ever happen to run into a former customer at an industry event or conference, this is a perfect opportunity to get a better understanding of why they are no longer a customer. It could simply be a pricing issue, but maybe it's deeper than that. Perhaps the product just didn't meet their standards or the onboarding process was simply too long. But maybe there was something that falls under the marketing purview that you can help to change.

A marketing starter would make tweaks to the customer communication process, help to better highlight customer wins and stories, or simply get the mission out there to customers and share in their beliefs. All of these are things that can be learned and implemented from having a casual chat with a former customer.

You can even step up your game by hosting a customer luncheon or event where you can learn from them directly. I've seen this done brilliantly at a few different companies where customers are given a platform to discuss their innermost hopes and dreams while sharing best practices with each other in a laid back setting.

In most instances, representatives from the customer support, sales, and even executive teams are part of the programming to show customers that their time is valuable. It may be a big lift to pull an event together, but your participation and attendance in these events will help you quickly learn the business.

If you're fortunate enough to be part of a marketing team that has a dedicated customer marketing leader, learning from your customers will be even easier. Lean on this leader to spill all the good customer gossip that will help you learn more about the business and how their perspectives and habits impact your role.

> **TIP 9:**
> Dig up all the customer marketing materials your company has created in the past. Read, watch, or listen to them—then talk to the content creators to learn more.

Customer marketing may have already compiled a bunch of case studies, testimonials, and even customer videos for you to dive into. Heck, they may already have events like the ones I mentioned earlier. No one else besides sales or customer success knows the customers better than these folks. And if you're the one in charge of customer marketing at your company, well, you're on your own, kid!

Just kidding! You can also use the tips above.

## No One Is Going to Train You

I'm not going to sugarcoat this: No one is going to train you when you're a marketing starter. There's not another soul around on Marketing Island, remember?

No one is going to show you the ropes beyond how to access your email, where to find marketing documents, and where the water cooler or—if you work for a hip tech startup—where the kombucha fridge is located.

This can be a little scary for the faint of heart.

No one—not your boss, colleagues, or counterparts—is going to give you everything you need to do your job right. They may offer their support when they can, but it's on you to know what you know and learn what you need to learn. That's just the nature of a starter role and something you should be prepared for.

Some of you might be shocked to walk into a new role and not find a thoughtful training plan laid out—but don't be.

Your new manager is not trying to mislead you or set you back. They are relying on you to have the wherewithal to plot your role's trajectory and ask the right questions to get the answers you need as you train yourself on the fly.

Yes, you heard me right. You must train *YOURSELF,* and you need to learn to do it quickly. If this is something you're not comfortable with, then starter marketing will certainly be a challenge. If you expect to be spoon-fed your daily schedule and training courses, then you will be in trouble.

In fact, it's good practice to train yourself in some capacity for any professional role. It's really all about taking initiative, and I would argue that true starters overflow with the do-whatever-it-takes kind of attitude.

In my experience, my managers have always equipped me with the tools (we'll get into tools a little later) and support I need but have never trained me on the tasks and tactics specific to my role.

Why, you may ask? Because they have been starter roles—roles that required me to write the script and, of course, train myself. I had to find ways to learn what was needed for my role on my own.

Of course, my managers and counterparts were always more than willing to assist by making introductions to people who could support my processes and explaining the ins and outs of the business, but it was up to me to stitch it all together.

Imagine that you are the first graphic designer hired onto a small marketing team. You may report to a marketing leader that hopefully has some design chops, but let's be honest, she hired you to be the expert and get the design program off the ground. You shouldn't expect your new manager to train you on anything sans the basic brand guidelines. She is counting on you to set the bar and deliver.

More likely than not, your design skills will outshine those of your manager, so you'll be teaching her! (I'll dig into more about being the teacher in chapter five.)

You'll also find ways to connect with your peers and across teams to learn how your role fits in the organization. You'll think of challenging questions to ask your manager and get the answers you need. You'll develop processes and procedures that will set the script for your role. You'll be the one who creates the training for your team in the future.

Remember the professional group you just joined on LinkedIn or met in person from a few sections ago? Well, surprise! More likely than not, they'll offer some sort of professional training sessions or seminars you can attend. These sessions are a great way to check two of your marketing starter boxes: get your networking game on while you train amongst your peers.

Jump on your association's calendar and see what training sessions make sense for you in your current role and sign up. It may cost money, but the ROI will be massive, especially if you receive some sort of certificate you can hang on your mother's refrigerator.

And yeah, you'll get to be one of those allstars with a long series of post-nominal initials next to their name in their email signature and on their business cards. No, that's not your game? I get it, you're more into it for the refined skill set and résumé power—so am I.

**TIP 10:**

Get through your basic business training, then ask for more. Set meetings with your peers and other managers to extend your training beyond what was assigned on day one.

The bottom line is, when you're coming into a marketing starter role, don't expect grand training procedures to get you up to speed. Expect that you will need to figure out what you need to learn and how to get trained. If you set the bar here, any training specific to your role will be a pleasant surprise.

## Dive into the Product Deep End

In order to properly market your company, you must learn the company's products to the best of your ability. You should know what your company sells, how it works, and, most importantly, the problem that it solves for the customer. I absolutely believe that it doesn't matter what you sell - which I'll go over in more detail later —but you should still know the product inside and out.

Imagine there was a big trade show coming up in your industry called Software X-FUTURE. And let's say that right before Software X-FUTURE two of your top salespeople came down with the flu and couldn't make it to Vegas for the show, and the only person left to staff was you. You pack your bags and stock up on 5-hour ENERGY to make it through the next three days. But what are you going to say when expo-goers pick up a pen and squishy ball and ask, "So what do you guys do?" Will you be able to rise to the occasion and give an elevator pitch and product overview that would make your CEO proud? Or will you get tongue-tied and pee your pants?

This trade show stage fright is only one of the many reasons you should learn what products your business sells. Doing your job to your fullest potential should be the top reason, and as marketing starters, we should all have a strong desire to strive for maximum effort. The question is: how difficult is it to understand your business's products?

Consumer products are super easy to grasp—whether it's a mobile app or tangible goods—because you can get your own hands on them and try them out. You can also talk to your friends and survey customers to see what they think. But, as you start to venture into B2B, learning the products can prove to be more difficult.

Imagine if the Salesforce workforce didn't use Salesforce, but instead some other CRM. The sales team would not be able to speak from personal experience about its functionality or superiority. What if the Zoom team used Google Hangouts? I think you get my point.

Of course, these companies have their own workforce using their tools. So if you worked there, you would be able to test and tinker before you started your programs. It is so much easier to learn the products when you're actively using them.

When I was with Dialpad, this helped a ton. Dialpad gave everyone within the company an instance of each tool to use in our day-to-day work. The product knowledge that came from personal use made it easy to talk to customers, partners, or whomever else about what Dialpad did.

What about more B2B services that you don't use directly? When I worked with Vendini, this was a challenge I had to overcome. The platform wasn't used internally, so I had to learn it in other ways. Finding your own way to use the product or service, even if you don't use it for your job, is one of those ways.

**TIP 11:**

Find ways of interacting with the product or engineering teams to grasp the product; perhaps your company is hosting a training session you can attend. Or, you can set some time on the calendar for a deeper dive.

This is great for software, but what about a service or a highly technical product for a niche market? For example, B2B consulting for pharma research scientists is tricky to conceptualize. There isn't a tool you can use day-to-day or a system you can log into to play around with. You have to rely on more keen methods of deducing what the product actually is.

It's hard to market a product you don't use or innately understand. In those cases, you'd need to depend on the product teams. You'll need to be more in-depth with your internal discussions and interviews with customers. You'll need to map out the business process in some sort of flow chart so that you can get a full understanding. And, of course, you'll rely heavily on the sales and business development teams to teach you the ways of the service.

It is possible to market any product, but you need to spend the time to know your strengths in the industry, product, or specific market. If you've been hired to help promote one of those highly-technical niche roles without previous experience, know this: You are going to need to devote a significant amount of time to learn the products or service while you're getting started. I'd never discourage you from taking on a role like this, however, you need to be prepared for the significant challenge it will be if you do not have any previous domain expertise in what you will be marketing.

## Understand the Competition and Know Your Differentiators

After clearly defining the company's why (which often aligns with their vision statement) and getting a grasp on business operations and products, the next step is to quickly ramp up your understanding of the company's competition and differentiators—i.e. what sets you apart.

Imagine being at a networking event, sipping on a cocktail, making your rounds when your next encounter asks, "So what sets your company apart from [insert competitor name here]?" You should be able to answer with your company's why statement, and follow up with a few top differentiators to support your case and where your company fits within the landscape.

If your company was truly one of a kind, it sure would make your job as a marketer easy, right? Your messaging could be as simple as, "Hey, we're the only supplier in town! You have to buy from us, so buy! Duhhh...."

Odds are you don't work for a global monopoly that has an overwhelming stronghold in the market, so you're going to have to be more creative with your marketing than that. The fact is, competition is the reason marketing exists and why we have jobs. So be thankful for your competition, because they make your job more interesting, especially when you win by marketing your differentiators.

When you are first learning the business, no one expects you to put together a full-fledged competitive analysis, but it's important to get a brief survey of your business's competitive landscape and differentiators because you are not the only game in town.

To figure out who your competitors are, I recommend pinging your colleagues—especially the sales and customer service teams—as a first step. They will always have a good pulse on what competitors your company is up against. Start a list and update it frequently.

Second, I would turn to your fancy internet machine to search for competitors who might be unknown to your colleagues. You'd be surprised to see that near competitors are sometimes missed. Also, spend some time on industry news sites and conference sites to scope out your competition's activity.

Researching your competitors not only helps you learn the differences between your products and services but also shows you how they market themselves. When researching your competitors, you'll stumble across blog posts, social media profiles, articles, advertisements, and sponsorships your competitors are using to capture new customers and drive demand.

Steal their ideas. These examples can drum up some excellent channels for your marketing plans.

> **TIP 12:**
> Use your personal profiles to sign up for competitor newsletters and promos and follow them on social media. Also, visit their website to get served advertisements and watch their webinars to scrape their marketing tactics.

Ask your product marketers to share any complete content they have created. They should have tons for you to look over. During my time at Dialpad, the product marketers took this very seriously. They had one-sheets, explainers, and videos with intricate details and talking points about how the company differentiated itself from competitors; business communications is a cutthroat space!

The dedication of resources was directly influenced by the competitive nature of the business telecommunications market. Many big players and tons of smaller ones made for Dialpad's vast competitive landscape. Thankfully, all of this fantastic work was already completed by the time my role at Dialpad was created. So, I was able to find this content in the company's hard drive and study up to get a good understanding of the company's competitive advantages.

I have worked in media, ticketing, parking, real estate, and telecommunications, just to name a few. While all the companies in those spaces use common marketing practices, the where, when, who, and how they target prospective and existing customers varies greatly by industry. You can easily learn the where, when, who and how for your marketing plans by paying close attention to your competitors.

# CHAPTER 3

## THE THREE-PHASE APPROACH

If you can't describe what you are doing as
a process, you don't know what you're doing.

–W. Edwards Deming
Engineer, statistician, professor,
author, lecturer, and management consultant

E very great story has a beginning, a middle, and an end. So
does starter marketing, with one small caveat—there's never
really an end, only starting over again.

In every role I've had in my career, no matter how big or small, I
have used a three-phase marketing starter approach once I have
learned the business. Whether building marketing programs from
scratch or taking over where someone else left off, I have found that
this approach works well when I'm initially planning for my role—
or the department, if I'm leading it.

It's a 30-, 60-, or 90-day plan that can be used when compiling a
grand marketing plan for the first year of your new job. In this chapter, I'll get into the details about my three-phase approach and how
it can work in any marketing role at any level.

## Phase 1: Assess and Investigate

Put on your best trench coat and grab your detective kit, because the first phase is to assess the current state of marketing within the company and how your role fits in. Part of your assessment is actually covered in the last chapter, where you spend time learning the business. However, the next step is to dig into the status of the marketing department.

Like conjuring up marketing ghosts from the past, the first task a marketing starter should do is to take a deep dive into the dark abyss and inventory of all the elements of the company that may have an impact on their role.

In my previous roles as marketing leader, I needed to take inventory on everything marketing touched, from sales collateral to conference premiums, blog posts to lead generation forms. I wanted to get a good understanding of everything marketing had created to date and its freshness.

What do I mean by freshness, you ask? Take case studies, for example. Sure, your company has a dozen great case studies with great takeaways from top customers, but how old are they? Were they published more than five years ago? Are the customers even customers anymore? If they're not, and the studies are outdated, this should be noted and fast-tracked for updates or taken out of the arsenal ASAP.

> **TIP 13:**
>
> To take inventory, create a spreadsheet of all marketing outputs. Then add columns for the statuses that work for you, like "freshness."

Download a template of marketing
outputs at themarketingstarter.com.

I also like to spend time taking inventory of current processes that affect marketing. Realistically, most of the processes will exist between marketing and sales, but there are other internal processes you'll want to seek to understand.

Marketing requests are a big one. How does the sales team request help from marketing, and how are those requests best prioritized? Lesson #1 in managing your relationship with sales is partnering with the sales leader so they can help you prioritize requests so your team doesn't get inundated. How about training? Is your role involved in sales enablement at all? If so, you need to lean on your sales counterpart to help coordinate and make sure that salespeople attend the training.

Throughout the assess and investigate phase, I like to constantly scan for the marketing department's key internal and external relationships and influencers. I ask myself questions like:

- How involved is upper management in marketing decisions?
- How does the current sales/marketing relationship feel?
- Are there key vendors you need to keep tabs on?

You might have already spent time on the marketing tool kit assessment when you were first onboarding, but it's imperative to get a grasp on all of the tools the marketing department has at its disposal. What CRM tools do they use (like Hubspot or Salesforce)? Do they use any automation tools (like Pardot or Marketo)? Email applications (like Constant Contact or Mailchimp)? Adobe Creative Suite? Hootsuite?

The list goes on and on and on, but it's good for you to have an idea of what tools exist in your sandbox today and how the company and your marketing department linked all of them together.

Lastly, make a wish list of tools you think would be most helpful for the department and your specific role (if they don't already exist) —tools like Outreach's email sequence builder or Demandbase's ABM platform. Be prepared to back up your reasoning to get them added to the budget if they're not free by building a solid business case. (We'll talk about budgeting in chapter six.)

That stuff ain't cheap!

> **TIP 14:**
> Sketch a quick bubble map or flowchart to see how all the marketing tools work together in your company and what triggers them. Look for gaps and tweak the workflow in a way that works for you.

Who handles your monthly newsletter? Who is responsible for creating sales collateral? Who is on call to organize conference sponsorships?

Whether you're leading your marketing team or not, you must know who champions the big marketing functions within your team. When you're learning the business, there should be plenty of time to get an understanding of who is responsible for what when you're learning everyone's roles. Take good notes so you know how each team member fits into the marketing puzzle and what they do to keep the processes flowing.

When I came into my first director role, I asked all my team reports to create a list of all the tasks they handled. We then covered those in a one-on-one to help me get an understanding of team responsibilities and alignment. I had them pop their tasks into a spreadsheet where they ranked each task from most important to least, and included the percentage of time they spent on each task on a weekly basis. I also asked them to highlight how favorable (how much they enjoyed or liked doing) each task was by labeling high, low, or neutral.

| RANK | TASK | TIME % | FAVORABILITY |
|------|------|--------|--------------|
| 1. | Newsletter | 25% | High |
| 2. | Blogs | 20% | Neutral |
| 3. | Conference Planning | 25% | Low |
| 4. | Develop Collateral | 15% | Neutral |
| 5. | Social Media | 15% | High |

**TIP 15:**
Create a simple task sheet where you can see each team member's list of duties. This will help you better understand what they favor doing and how much of their time is spent doing it.

It is a fantastic exercise for your reports to dig deep into their task list to get an understanding of how they spend their time weekly. Many of them may have never thought about how much time they allot to each task or how important each is to their role, so this gives them a better idea of their contribution to the team. As a marketing leader, it is also a great exercise for you in a few key ways:

1. It helps to understand what each person does and how they spend their time.
2. You'll unearth any task overlaps between team members or glaring gaps.
3. You have the ability to immediately shift tasks from one team member to another based on demand or favorability.
4. You'll be able to prioritize and align the team on time allotment.

While this exercise can go pretty deep, you can create a table of your own when onboarding and learning everyone's responsibilities, even if you're a junior marketing professional.

Finally, once you take inventory, understand processes, learn key relationships, map out your tools, and learn your team's roles, you can complete a quick gap analysis. A good place to start is to understand why you were hired in the first place. The company and the department saw an immediate need for someone in your role, so ask yourself:

- What major function gap does your role fill?
- What processes need to be set or changed?
- What tools do you need to do your job the best you can?

Another great way to determine gaps is to ask during your interview (which I touched on in chapter two). Ask questions like, "What can marketing do today that would make your job better?" or "What marketing resources do you need to improve your output?" Remember, everyone in the company is a customer of marketing in some way, so there is a never-ending list of gaps to fill.

Don't let this overwhelm you; in fact, as a marketing starter, it should excite you. Those gaps are the reason you got the job in the first place.

## Phase 2: Organize and Build

Assessment done! Onto the next step, but let me tell you a quick story about my lovely wife, Michelle.

My wife is what one might call a fashionista who is completely infatuated with shoes. She has shoes upon shoes upon shoes.

When we first moved in together, shortly after getting engaged, we went through the painstaking exercise of making room for my clothes in the master bedroom closet. I found it challenging to hold back my snarky comments about the sheer amount of space she devoted to her precious shoe collection.

She literally had multiple colors of the same shoe so she could "have options" to go along with the million outfit combinations she could possibly put together. I'm sure many shoe fanatics out there can identify with her.

To make space for me in the closet, she finally agreed to let a few pairs go, so I helped her take inventory and get organized. We discovered that she had multiple pairs she hadn't worn in years and some she purchased and never wore at all! This was unfathomable to me, but to her, this varied collection was very important.

Once she determined which shoes would stay and which would go, we finally had enough space for just a few of my things.

Much like making space in a significant other's closet for the very first time, you must take the time to organize the marketing closet, both metaphorically and physically. Almost every company has a daunting closet hidden somewhere, where mysterious one-sheets, estranged pamphlets, and outdated laptop stickers lay dormant in its nooks and crannies. But the marketing closet is not only physical inventory—it's all the digital documents, processes, and repositories your company has created over the years.

Whether your marketing assets are stashed away digitally in Google Drive or in the aforementioned closet, as a marketing starter, you need to get all your marketing affairs in order. Your rigorous assessment and investigation have now put you in a place where you can swap your detective hat for a construction helmet and start building.

A big part of getting organized and building is to create new systems for you, your marketing team, and specific projects. I'm talking about creating marketing request forms to better funnel and filter sales requests, utilizing calendars to manage content and conferences, and setting recurring meetings between you and the product team to stay on top of the product pipeline.

If you're a Type A person, who is borderline obsessive compulsive like me, you get a little giddy thinking about this organization phase. You get to be methodical in planning systems, but be sure to also keep them simple so the triggers that get your little marketing machine in action are easily understandable by all the constituents who use them.

For those who are not so organized, I highly recommend you step up your organization game, because navigating the treacherous waters of marketing starter seas can be difficult if you don't get organized.

This is the rule of the minimum viable product, or MVP. This is a term known all too well in startup culture. Eric Ries, entrepreneur and author of *The Lean Startup,* famously defined the MVP as the version of a new product which allows a team to collect the maximum amount of validated learning about customers with the least effort.

In other words, it's the most simple version of a product that you can produce with limited resources that someone will buy. Or, in the case of a marketer, a program that is usable.

Much like the MVP of a new SaaS platform or mobile app, your new marketing programs should be built scrappy, but good enough to be used in the real world.

Let's take the marketing-adored and sales-disdained marketing request form, for example. Prior to your arrival, the marketing team was facilitating marketing requests from the sales team on a one-off basis, usually in the form of a short email or the occasional desk stop-by.

Once the task was roughly explained, the team would jot it down on a sticky note and place it somewhere on their desk to get to when they had time. And before they knew it, their desks were buried in sticky notes with requests that had no prioritization or timeline.

How could anyone ever expect to get to those tasks in any sort of rational order or cadence? I was once at a company that functioned, or should I say dysfunctioned, just like this, causing the marketers to feel overwhelmed and the sales team to be left in the dark, wondering if their request would ever be fulfilled.

The simple solution was creating a task request protocol beginning with a marketing request form. I created a basic form that allowed the salesperson to offer the level of detail the marketing team needed to correctly prioritize and execute the task. Sure, sales hated it at first, but once the system started to flow and they saw the results, they bought in.

In this scenario, I was desperately trying to get the company's marketing initiatives back on track, so I was very intentional about the form and got buy-in from other managers across the organization. This helped to ensure that their teams would use the form and not go rogue and swing by my marketing team members' desks asking for one-off favors.

**TIP 16:**

Once your form or other simple marketing system is live, send a company-wide email (or to whomever your internal customers are) letting everyone know about the form's importance and process.

Download the marketing request form at
themarketingstarter.com.

Since I was trying to tame this wild process, completed forms were funneled to me, and then I assigned each project to the appropriate marketer on the team. Once assigned, the marketer would confirm and reach out to the requester directly to get started on the project.

Simple, right? Processes like this may seem like overkill, but if your department or project lacks serious organization, these systems can be extremely helpful.

Now that you have your tasks inbound, it's time to organize them and your projects. There are dozens of tools that will help you get your adorable little marketing ducks in a row, but ideally, you should use the tool that your marketing department uses. If they don't have a collective task management tool, this is where you as a marketing starter can have some valuable input.

My favorite tools to use are Asana, Trello, and even Jira from time to time. Asana is fantastic for organizing a multitude of tasks at a project and department level and gives users the ability to see beyond their nearsighted list to what is happening within the team as a whole. It also gives great managerial insights into the team's progress.

In a previous director role, I shared my Asana profile with my manager (the COO) and called out specifics in our one-on-ones. It gave her all the visibility she needed to track what marketing was doing on the daily.

> **TIP 17:**
> Visibility and transparency are key. Whatever task manager you use, be sure your team and management can collaborate and see the workloads.

Marketing starters should also look into other tools that will help streamline their processes. Perhaps your company's CRM is broken and it's time for an upgrade, or your new website project calls for a more advanced marketing automation solution. These new tools should support the new systems that you set in place for your role and project demands.

In this phase, I like to use the analogy of building a restaurant kitchen. Before you can cook, you need to clean your new restaurant space, map out where all of the equipment will live, and have a menu in place. The industrial refrigerator should be close to the walk-in cooler, the wash bins should be near the dishwasher and drying rack, and the cookware should be hung next to stoves and ovens (and always put back in the same place where it belongs).

You'll need to stock the fridge and cooler with all the supplies to make the dishes on the menu, and the cooks will need to learn the recipes. You'll need a process in place that begins when the server gives the order to the kitchen and culminates when the kitchen gives the completed order to the server. Once all that is organized and built out, then and only then can you open the doors to the hungry guests and start cooking.

### Phase 3: Measure and Scale

One summer I took on the project of my very first motorcycle rebuild. Yes, in case you couldn't tell from my Triumph example from before, I'm a bit of a motorcycle fan. Earlier in the year, I purchased a 1980 Honda CM400T that I found on Craigslist for $1,000. It was in decent shape, but more importantly, it ran strong.

My mission was to completely rebuild the bike from the frame up and turn it into a little cafe racer to whip through the hills of the Bay Area. I spent months researching how to build and modify it—placing what had to have been a hundred orders for parts. When all was said and done, the bike came together beautifully. But the question was, would it run? I had assessed, I had built, and now it was time to fire it up. Key switch on. Clutch pulled in. And, fortunately for me, it started right up.

Much like how I built my little cafe racer motorcycle, your three-phase marketing approach is always put to the test in the end —phase three.

This is where you implement your long-researched and constructed bounty and pray that it works. Once you complete your assessment and finish your organization and building, it's time to fire up your marketing machine and see what happens. If you've done it right, it should start right up and roll smoothly down the road. If you've missed a step or created a faulty process, it will sputter and need some tuning.

**TIP 18:**
Don't be afraid to fail or to sputter like an old motorcycle. Your systems will never be perfect in the first round. Be prepared to accept feedback and quickly iterate.

One of the biggest mistakes I see marketers make is spending all the resources and all the manpower to create fool-proof marketing programs, only to never know if any of the company's results can be attributed to them. Proper measuring and tracking are key to the marketing starter mentality because, as a marketing starter, you need to be able to quickly assess your results, make iterations, and scale.

You simply can't do this without any tracking or measurement practices in place. Your number one measure should be your return on marketing investment or ROMI, but I'll go more deeply into setting your measures for ROMI in chapter eight. Here, I want to stress the need for you to, at the very least, build some basic systems that will help you track how your work is performing beyond clicks, likes, or other vanity metrics.

Following phase three, believe it or not, the journey isn't over. Next you must focus on rapid growth. The key is to make sure that your first three phases have been tested and executed properly and that your systems are built to handle the growth that will come. We'll cover this idea in more detail in chapter ten.

In case you are wondering, yes that little old motorcycle did fire right up—on the first try! And boy, did that ever feel good. All the hard work and hours devoted to the overhaul and she worked. It did require a lot of tuning to get it running smoothly, just like your marketing processes and systems. But don't worry, this can all be done over time.

## Don't Forget the Low-Hanging Fruit

Ever heard of the Brazilian pirapitinga fish? If not, take a moment and search for it on YouTube because it's a perfect analogy for this point and this overused cliché. Basically, it's a tropical freshwater fish that lives in the Amazon and is well-known for its unique talent— the fish is a pro at leaping out of the water and grabbing small tasty fruits dangling from trees just above the water.

Like a pirapitinga fish, you must take little leaps to claim your low-hanging fruit. Within the amassed tasks for new starters, there are plenty of big, long-term projects that will take a ton of brain power and hours, as well as small, simple tasks that can be knocked out while working on big projects.

Remember when your mom said, "It's the little things that count?" Well, she wasn't wrong, especially about making your company happy while you're doing more in-depth marketing lab work.

When doing your investigation, learn what tasks are your low-hanging fruit—tasks, which can be completed quickly yet will make everyone super happy. Perhaps it's a one-sheet, landing page, or client thank-you gift basket campaign. No matter what it is, cross them off your list rapidly and diligently and watch the faith in your work build. You'll notice that it will be easier for you to make the case for your longer-term projects if your company can see tangible results from smaller projects you have done that demonstrate your hustle and solve real problems.

> **TIP 19:**
> Compile a list of quick wins and make time to complete them in your first 30, 60, and 90 days. Including some that are cross-functional will always help to strengthen your plans.

The key to your success here is to not get so overwhelmed with all the little things that nothing big ever gets done. Proper planning based on your bandwidth and proper communication with your manager are imperative. Take care of every piece of low-hanging fruit, otherwise you'll be spinning your wheels on the bigger stuff. You'll need to find that fine balance between what is most important to the business and what will make certain people happy.

# CHAPTER 4

## A TEAM OF MARKETING ACES

I hire only people who are smart, scrappy, and sensational.

–Rebecca Biestman
CMO, Reputation.com

During the regular season, a Major League Baseball team has thirteen pitchers on the active roster—five starters and seven to eight relief pitchers. Typically, the team manager sets a five-man rotation of starting pitchers which includes his best pitchers, also known as aces, at the beginning of the rotation.

Most of the time, the team only has one ace, but if they are lucky, they will have two or more if they make the right trades. I remember back to the 2003 Chicago Cubs season, when the team was known for their stellar pitching. Everyone believed they were destined for a championship, but that championship didn't come for another thirteen years. Nevertheless, that 2003 team was known for the two amazing ace pitchers on their staff: Kerry Wood and Mark Prior.

That year, they combined for 32 game wins and 511 strikeouts. And at age 20, Wood tied the major league record with 20 strikeouts in a single game. *Sports Illustrated* featured the pair on a cover that year with the title "Chicago Heat"—both of them held a baseball that was in flames. Wouldn't we all love to have aces like that on our team?

They were revered by all as the dynamic duo that would break the team's infamous curse and lead all of the Cubs fandoms to glory. To much chagrin, these two were not the saving grace for the Cubs, who that year ended up falling just short of attending their first World Series in nearly sixty years.

I'm totally geeking out on my favorite team right now, but just like in baseball, your team of marketers will have their ups and downs, and individual staff members will come and go. There will be champions and there will be duds, but you need to learn to be that player coach who can find the right talent for your team and retain it.

This is even more important in today's job market, where, according to Gallup, employees only stick around for an average of two years. No matter the role you're in, you must find ways to keep your team engaged. Empowering your team to be marketing starters will help keep them more engaged, more efficient, and more loyal.

**Define Your Specialties**

There are dozens upon dozens of specialties in today's marketing landscape. From product to content to digital to communications to branding, it's important as a marketing starter to know what specialties you will need in order to round out your team or find where you fit in your team. More importantly, if you're a marketing leader, you'll need to know what roles you need and when to hire talented individuals to fill them.

Remember the T-shaped marketer that I referenced in chapter one? A team of T-shaped marketers who complement each other's skill sets is the kind of team you want to build.

The example I gave in chapter three about building a team task chart is a good place to start when mapping out prospective hires. I did this very thing in a director role. When I was hired, there was already one marketer in place, and I had one open role to fill. The current marketer was so used to wearing all the marketing hats that she was stretched super thin, and her task list was outrageous.

To figure out what type of skills I needed to fill the vacant role, I went to the task chart of my current marketer and noted the gaps and the types of tasks she favored the least. I also took into account her aptitude and experience for the tasks that were lagging. From there, we were able to build a list of necessary skills and requirements that we wanted from the next marketer that we hired.

> **TIP 20:**
> Lay out roles from the spectrum that are needed in your marketing department and describe how the roles inevitably morph over time.

Just like when you apply a three-phase approach in the early days with your company, you'll want to think about how to structure your team in phases to match your business and marketing plans. A lot of the planning here will come during your marketing growth phase, but you can, early on, make good estimations of the people you will need to round out your team.

Not every team's roles are the same. Some are all generalists, and some are more seasoned than the last. Some have very defined roles.

I have always been a fan of balancing my team's individual strengths and what they enjoy doing the most with what they want to be when they grow up (in their careers). I work with them to make them into champions of certain projects or facets of our marketing team.

With a small starter team, we all must collaborate on every project while laying out a spectrum in which individuals can be owners of their work. This tactic has worked really in my starter-oriented teams, no matter how big or small.

## Motivate and Grow

A big part of being a marketing starter is to empower yourself, but also to empower others around you, especially your team. Booker T. Washington once said, "If you want to lift yourself up, lift up someone else." This quote couldn't sum up this next section more beautifully.

If you're serving in a leadership role, it's your duty to constantly motivate your team and help them grow within their roles and the company.

I'm not going to pretend that I'm some sort of motivational expert; I'm merely a marketing one. However, there are piles of articles you can research to get tips on keeping your team motivated. You'll see things like "pay them what they're worth," "set clear goals," "don't micromanage," and "avoid useless meetings." While those are all great, I have a few strategies of my own that have worked really well from the marketing perspective.

First, I believe it is imperative to have an open communication strategy with your team. In recent roles, I encouraged my team to be accessible through multiple communication channels during work hours. Whether chatting or texting, we were always on call for each other's needs. This is critical if your team does any work-from-home hours or participates in a hybrid work environment. I also set up a weekly team kickoff meeting in addition to my individual one-on-ones with each team member.

Beyond the channels themselves, it's important that the team culture welcomes continuous feedback and suggestions. A consultative management style will really allow your team to flourish. These tactics have been effective at keeping my teams aligned and creating an open and productive communication style within the group.

**TIP 21:**
Create an online chat group for your marketing team or for specific projects, and make sure the chat is open on computers and phones during work hours so you can communicate easily with your team.

The second strategy is to encourage team advocacy. Whether or not you're in a leadership role, your team must feel like you have their backs. Certainly, marketing is responsible for its internal customers, but the team must always be advocates for each other.

Nothing will dismantle a team's morale faster than an environment in which members don't feel trusted. This is crucial if you are in a leadership role where you are responsible for propping up your team's accomplishments and advocating for them across departments and with upper management.

Many times, great marketing work can go unnoticed if it doesn't directly impact revenue, so advocating your amazing work can often be a challenge. That's where those tips to gain exposure in chapter two come in handy.

**TIP 22:**
Make your team feel as if there is as little hierarchy as possible to create a trusting environment. Always be willing to help out your team no matter how trivial the task and be a "get your hands dirty" kind of marketer.

The third strategy is to clearly communicate the why for your team. Not to beat a dead horse here, but as I referenced in chapter two, everything your team does should point back to your department's why, which is derived from your company's why.

Once you have a handle on your company's why, you can create one for your department and get your team's buy-in. The buy-in is the most important part, and as a marketing leader, it's your duty to get everyone on board.

Your why statement can vary greatly by department focus; it could be something as simple as, "Our marketing team exists to establish trust and rapport with prospects" or "We believe in top-tier marketing services for our internal customers." You'll want to find a why statement or mission that works best for your team, but be sure to keep it simple so your team members can recite it easily from memory.

**Plot Your Trajectory**

We're all familiar with the airline safety instructions to secure our oxygen masks before helping others. While it may not be so obvious, flight attendants ask you to secure your mask first so you don't pass out when trying to help someone else who can't help themselves. Then you're both down for the count!

The same goes for your personal career planning as a marketing starter. As you're helping to motivate and nurture your team, you should learn to secure your own motivation first, because if you're not happy where you are in the company, your drive will wane and your team will notice.

Is your manager not doing a great job keeping you motivated and helping you plan your career trajectory within the company? That's okay, because you're a marketing starter, and you have already taken the steps to motivate yourself. You'll need to create your own pathway and be open about it with your manager.

During one of my times serving as director of marketing, I reported directly to the COO, who reported to the CEO. The organization was very flat, so I took it upon myself to talk through my trajectory desires with the COO during my review.

I told her that within the next year I saw myself moving into a senior director role and ultimately to VP of marketing, all while under her wing. I created a plan that showed the growth of my responsibility and how my team's organization chart changed over time. This did two-fold: showed my expectations and goals professionally and showed my dedication to the company by my desire to stay and grow over time.

> **TIP 23:**
> Jot down how you see yourself growing within your company and judge the feasibility before you start looking elsewhere. There may be a ton of opportunities right where you already are!

Your personal trajectory doesn't have to stay within company walls, but while you are still with the company, it is important not to get distracted by the new, shiny job before you even get settled. You can plan for your next role outside the company while keeping your work and team on point in your current role. This is achieved by making sure you never forget how important your work and time are to your overall career success.

The easiest way to do this is to have a great attitude, do quality work, and be absolutely grateful while in your current role. Whether you're serving six months or six years, you don't want to burn a bridge by seeming distracted by your career ladder climb or doing poor quality work. If you grow beyond what your company can offer you, be candid about this internally, and they will be likely to advocate for you when you're ready to take the next step.

At the end of the day, you'll need to manage your own expectations and be realistic in order to build the best team. You may not get top-notch workers or land people who truly buy into your mission, but that's okay. You're a marketing starter, and you can roll with the punches, even if they come in the form of employee turnover. Once you have your team of marketing starters working with you, however, your sticky mentality should bond you even closer and accelerate your success.

# CHAPTER 5

## LESSONS IN MULTI-DIRECTIONAL MANAGEMENT

The conventional definition of management
is getting work done through people, but real
management is developing people through work.

–Agha Hasan Abedi
Founder, Bank of Credit and Commerce International

There are thousands of books you can order on Amazon that will teach you just as many approaches to management. There are courses, seminars, and peer groups all focused on making us better managers.

With all the tips and tactics out there, there is no magic wand that will make you a better manager or make your employees and bosses easier to manage. And, as tough as this may be to swallow, managing can be an even greater challenge for marketing starters. The increased visibility, accountability, and sensitivity add a lot to the starter challenge.

When I think of the multi-directional management that marketing starters face, I am reminded of Rich, a good friend of mine and pro marketer whomI have known since college. He has become all too familiar with the challenges of managing up, down, and across during his marketing tenure.

When he was first getting his start in marketing, he had a boss who seemed completely out of his element and lacked the utmost important skills of being a supportive leader. Rich was new to his industry and didn't know the platform or business all that well, so he had to circumvent his boss and do as any good marketing starter would—rely on colleagues within the organization to learn. *I recommend doing this carefully, by the way, so as not to upset the dynamic you have with management.*

His counterparts knew how things functioned because most of them had been around the block a few times. They broke it down for him, and because they sat in an open office environment, Rich was able to listen in and figure out ways to incorporate what he heard into his repertoire.

Rich applied a lateral bypass to get the help he needed to be successful in his start. He relied on hearing, applying, reshaping, and reusing real-life scenarios from co-workers to make it work for him.

Often, Rich felt like he could do his boss's job—like we all do from time to time. His boss had a hard time managing the vast range of personalities and needs within his dynamic team. This, unfortunately, fostered a lot of resentment toward his boss within the team.

Rich even found that his boss's lack of acumen and empathy for the team often escalated into arguments, but Rich knew he had to suck it up and find a way of respecting his boss's way of problem-solving. It was a huge ego check for him. Even though he didn't agree, he had to fall in line, which can be cumbersome for a marketing starter.

Rich found it was more fruitful and a much better use of his energy to focus on changing his own methods rather than trying to change those of his boss. After all, it's not his job to change his boss's mind. He gave his management team his profound perspective, so all he could do was wait and hope they would overcome their stubbornness.

What Rich learned from his frustrating encounters with hardheaded managers early on is that he needed to come to the table with real solutions, as opposed to adding to the problems.

As you can see from Rich's story, there's no better role in which you learn management skills than as a marketer. In my marketing starter roles, I have reported to VPs, COOs, CMOs, CROs, and CEOs. I've had junior and senior marketers report to me and collaborated with executives, VPs, directors, and managers in other departments. I've even had the ability to partner with senior leaders at customer companies and large industry organizations.

Anyone who has ever been in a starter role can attest to the amount of cross management that has to be done. When you're responsible for building something new, there are a myriad of stakeholders across the company who look to you to be the chief of your project and manage them. Whether above you or below you, you're the one in the driver's seat, responsible to manage it all.

## How Starters Manage

Now that you know the business inside and out, set your processes, and assembled your team of aces—the next big unanswered question is: How does a marketing starter manage? In professional settings, we have all heard how we need to manage up, down, and across departments, but marketing starters should be able to do this with a little flair.

My style has always been to treat others how *they* want to be treated—the Platinum Rule. But I don't do this by simply being nice or by treating them all differently. I treat my reports as fellow marketing starters who are building great things from scratch, who don't have a ton of time, and who need to train themselves on the fly and do it all with limited resources.

You know, with some damn patience and mutual respect for what they are doing! Not to say that I have never received this in my many jobs—I most certainly have—but not everyone within a company knows what it takes to be a starter in a support role like marketing. You should.

> **TIP 24:**
> Make your management style transparent. Don't surprise your reports; rather, set expectations early and give them tips for managing up to you.

Everyone wants to be managed differently. Watch and observe and understand what your employees' need in order to better manage them. Give them an easy task with a clear goal, but based on their knowledge and past comparisons. Let them do what they need to do to finish the job.

If your team member needs more hand holding, they may require a bit more detailed instruction. But instructions can be difficult to convey when you're writing the script as you go. It's hard to say, "If you see this, then do that," because in starter marketing, there are no set "ifs." There are no straight lines, which a lot of people may not grasp right away. Managing as a marketing starter isn't as easy as basic algebra. We need to make sure that our team members understand that starter marketing is chock-full of trial and error and that it's okay to fail.

A good marketing starter manager knows what they need in this world. They need people with a solid understanding of the basic marketing necessities, but need them to be starters themselves—to have the drive to run with tasks and complete them.

They must bring in people to support their weaknesses as a manager and as a marketer—people with complementary skills both major and minor—and to support the team.

Team chemistry is also super important, which can sometimes be hard to gauge in an interview, but chemistry will create freedom from micromanagement and the ability to finish team initiatives smoothly.

Thankfully, as a marketing starter, you understand these concepts well. You get it, so you should be able to manage your employees in the unique way that marketing starters should be managed.

Managing down in a starter role really isn't that difficult; it just takes clear expectation setting and tons of communication. I believe in always having open lines of communication with my team, no matter the channel, especially during crunch time on big projects. I want them to know I am there to support them and to be an advocate wherever possible.

## Create Real Accountability

Team accountability begins with piecing together the right team of marketing starters, which I covered in the previous chapter—but managing them is a whole other beast. I have always believed in a trust-oriented, consultative management style.

Your employees should be empowered and trusted to do their jobs to the highest degree of their ability without the need to micromanage. Now, that being said, in order to properly manage as a marketing starter, you need to create accountability for your team.

Accountability is your form of measurement for your team's outputs. Accountability is key to the success of your team operating as an internal service provider, and it's up to you as a marketing starter to set the tone. At the management level, you need to set the expectation for you and your team to be accountable to each other and your customers. If you are not a manager, you need to enforce accountability for yourself and your colleagues to reinforce your integrity.

Your team's accountability points back to the organization, and a well-oiled and highly organized team will naturally create internal accountability. The principal way I do this with my teams is through task management tools, meetings, spot check-ins, and reviews. Implementing a tool like Asana to manage your team's tasks will create that managerial and departmental visibility and create immediate accountability for everyone who uses it.

If tasks aren't getting completed, the entire team will see. It also serves as a great tool to keep track of the workload, and it's helpful for the entire team to see whether fellow team members are getting bogged down. During one gig, I took my team's task list to my COO almost weekly, and I walked her through the list for each team member at a high level so she had the executive visibility she needed.

The next layer of the tasty accountability cake is to take these task lists to your weekly team meeting.

You don't have a weekly team meeting, you say? Well, you should set one up!

If your team is doing any sort of agile or project-based marketing, a weekly meeting will help sync everyone up. I like to hold mine at 10:00 a.m. on Mondays, which gives my team enough time to get in and update their task statuses from the previous week, and, of course, get their morning coffee.

During the meeting, we go over the major projects as a whole, project sprint timelines, and hone important individual tasks. This time also gives team members a forum to voice their opinions and concerns about work for the coming week. Fantastic accountability!

> **TIP 25:**
> Create consistency and transparency within your team. Use documents and meetings to keep track and share what everyone is working on to create accountability.

As a marketing starter manager, I believe scheduling time individually with direct reports is important so you can give them a safe space to speak with you candidly. One-on-ones are excellent for this, but I also firmly believe that every manager should make themselves available to their employees at a moment's notice, not just during scheduled meeting times. An employee should never be caught off guard by how you view their work, their standing with the company, or the progression of the team. As a manager, you should always be offering your perspective on those things throughout the week, not just during scheduled one-on-one times.

I'm not going to rant about that though—off the soapbox.

In my meetings with my direct reports, I would ask them more general questions about their tasks and whether they had any issues to discuss. I also made sure to offer them constant feedback during these times, so there were no surprises come review time.

The bottom line is that accountability can be forced, but it shouldn't. It should be created through simple systems and open communication. When your team is held accountable, it will help you—as a marketing starter—build better, faster, and stronger systems and campaigns.

## Advocate, Evangelize, and Validate

Here comes the waterfall of positivity… are you ready?

When it comes to your work and your team's work, advocating, evangelizing, and validating are the best ways to ensure success. If you manage a stellar team of marketing aces, it can be very easy to stand up for them and be the sounding board for all that they do. After all, they are your little marketing starters in the making. How could you resist shouting how proud you are from the rooftops?

Shouting from the rooftops can be far more difficult to do if you're a marketing department of one, however. When pressure is mounting on all sides and your process feels at best sluggish, it can feel difficult to stand up and advocate for yourself.

But I encourage you to do so. Don't ever become the proverbial marketing whipping-person. You need to reach down inside for your voice and use it to advocate for yourself, especially if appreciation for your fabulous marketing efforts seems to be lacking.

If you are fortunate enough to have a team under you, you must showcase your team's accomplishments, and make sure people are aware of the great work that is happening. You must also demand that their needs are met and show them you have their backs no matter what. Not only will they appreciate you as a manager, but they will have better work output while building trust in the team you have built.

Having a spine really comes in handy.

## Cross-Departmental Collaboration

As I mentioned at the very beginning of this book, I believe marketing is an internal service provider to many customers within a company. Those customers are the counterparts in various departments across the organization, such as sales, customer support, executive staff, etc. So, your marketing tasks never end at your team's lone responsibilities. Marketing has arguably the most cross-departmental collaborative tasks and projects, and that collaboration is imperative to your success as a marketing starter.

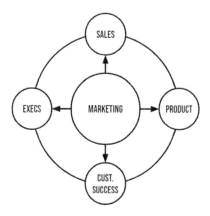

Managing your leadership counterparts in other departments should be as smooth and as respectful as managing your own team. You need them to buy in and communicate your marketing initiatives to their reports. The best way to do this is to be clear on the value proposition of your marketing efforts.

You need to show them why your new marketing initiative is impactful for their team. You need to make them care. Learn to speak their language while also leaning on the collaborative nature of your company as a whole. It's on you to get them to understand why your delivery is important or why your request for them is paramount.

Sometimes, you will run into roadblock after roadblock with other teams. It will seem that no matter how hard you try, you simply cannot get through to them or even elicit a response. It will seem disrespectful at times, but try not to take this personally. You must remember that your marketing initiatives are not seen as the top priority in other departments, even though your project may be bridging a gap between multiple departments in the company.

This is where that old saying, "The squeaky wheel gets the grease," comes into play. Follow up with emails, swing by their office, or schedule a meeting. Do what it takes to get them to take notice of your request.

If all else fails, don't hesitate to take up their lack of communication with your superior. This works really well if you need to hold their feet to the fire, but don't be a snitch! Don't go to your boss whining about the lack of support from the other teams; instead, mention that you are having difficulties and ask if they can help by offering a nudge. I have had to do this constantly in my marketing starter roles.

At Vendini, when my tasks were obscure to the rest of the company, I nearly had to beg at times to get support from other departments. My boss knew this, and he would ask me about statuses related to cross-department projects in our one-on-ones. He gladly offered his help to reach across, above my pay grade, to put pressure on other teams to fulfill my requests.

The key to this, of course, is always to handle the situation with grace. You never want to make it feel like you went around your colleague's back. Be sure that you have done everything in your power to keep the dialogue going with them before asking for that gentle nudge. If they are respectable, they'll understand, and hopefully be much better about their communication in the future.

You must build relationships and credibility with other teams. This will help you establish a reputation as someone who knows their stuff and follows through when they say they are going to do something. You know, that whole integrity thing. As long as you do that simple trust-building practice, you'll get what you need from other teams and establish the partnership you need to be successful.

Here's yet another place where there's no room for your ego. No one cares what successful company you came from or how important your projects were or even how smart you are. They care what you are working on now and how you collaborate with them.

> **TIP 26:**
> Make friends with the administrative assistants. They are the gatekeepers of the organization and can often help you out, especially if you're a department of one. Need a place to store your tradeshow booth? Your admin has the key to the closet. Need expo supplies shipped out on time? Well, guess who has access to the FedEx account.

Empathy is important. Put yourself in their shoes and never think that you're better or smarter than them. This is all the more reason to build cross-functional relationships within your company.

## Be the Teacher

In many of my marketing starter roles, I have lived in ambiguity, where the swim lanes of responsibility weren't always as clear to the rest of the company as they were to me. This was often apparent in two distinct ways.

First, the title and role were common, but how it functioned within the greater organization was unclear. And second, the title was abstract, which made it difficult to know how others were supposed to work alongside me.

I have also found that when you are partnered alongside counterparts who themselves have obscure roles, you may need to teach them how best to collaborate with your role. When I was working at Dialpad, one of my main internal customers was the head of business development.

The title, which in itself sounds very definitive, had a much deeper meaning that was lost on the company at times. His role, not to be confused with sales business development, was to drive strategic partnerships for the company by forming relationships with complementary technology and service companies.

A mouthful, right?

At the time I started working with him, he was a one-man show, formulating grand plans in his head while being in desperate need of marketing support. The man was savvy and moved quickly. He had me hit the ground running, looping me into partner calls and meetings and finding ways for me to help him on the marketing front.

Throughout this trial-by-fire, I applied my partnership skills to quickly build rapport with him and learn the intricacies of his business, but what was most important was that I helped to coach him in the ways of marketing. What was missing on his end was the understanding of how the marketing flow worked from his side of the business.

I had to ask him questions and help document how his partnerships, which were very nuanced, were formulated. Each one put their own demands on marketing, and I served as the point person. I spent a lot of time with him to help him understand the processes and we were able to create a sustainable workflow that plugged into the partner marketing plan.

> **TIP 27:**
> Patience is king when being the teacher. At times, teaching may be the most difficult part of your job. Hold meetings to delicately show your counterparts how to partner with you.

Throughout my career, I have had to apply the very same strategies as I did with Dialpad's head of business development to many other internals, especially executives. In fact, this may be the most common scenario: you, as a marketing professional, being the teacher.

Keep in mind that our executives are wise leaders, and they should be respected to the full extent, but you are the domain expert in your marketing starter role. They hired you to be the expert and should trust you to know how to build your programs best, so you will need to teach them the ins and outs of marketing and your role.

## Create Executive Transparency

Managing executives and their expectations may be one of the most difficult types of management scenarios you will ever face—far more difficult than managing your team and other departments combined. Typically, executives operate at a 30,000-foot view within the company and only occasionally swoop down to take a closer look. When they eventually do, it can often be all the way to the ground and deep into the weeds where no one wants them.

Unfortunately, there's really not much in between, and since marketing starters often find themselves in flatter organizations, learning to mitigate this with a keen sense of executive understanding can change your marketing world.

To do so, you must create clear and concise communication strategies that will give the executive team the transparency they need.

I will admit that I learned this lesson the hard way before I got it right. When working for startup companies, executives and founders are very involved in day-to-day operations and have a great deal to say about marketing, especially when it involves driving demand. So, part of your starter plan should include how you will present your plans and metrics to them. This is achieved with a variety of tactics:

- No matter the scope of the marketing specialization you

have, even if it would never call for it, write a damn marketing plan! You should be doing this for your own sanity at minimum, but more important than that, it gives your boss and executives tangible plans for your role. How impressive would it be for a content marketer to draft a brief marketing plan laying out all the details of the content strategy for the year? The execs would be blown away! Not only will a marketing plan help you stay organized and make it look like you have your act together, but it will also help your manager write their own business plan—one which undoubtedly they have to do and need to run all the way to the top of the company. As a manager, I always like to task my team with writing short, one-page marketing plans for their role to get an idea of their organization skills and test our team alignment. It's such a fantastic exercise!

- Go beyond your one-on-ones and quarterly reviews and schedule project check-in meetings with your superiors. Take the initiative to involve your boss or executives in your projects, even if it is an arm's length, by calling project check-in meetings with them. These can be short, no more than 30 or 45 minutes, but give yourself enough time to go over your drafted agenda and call back to your marketing plan to show off your progress. Be sure to add time for questions and, of course, comments and opinions. We all know how opinionated executives can be! The overall goal here is to give them a quick and easily digestible view of your efforts. If they have time to attend the meeting, they will certainly appreciate it. If they can't make it, they at the very least nod the initiative.

- When projects are all said and done, bosses and executives eagerly await results. It's very easy to appease them because you, the savvy marketing starter, have been planning on giving them the low down this whole time. Similar to the check-in meeting, call another meeting or draft a quick slide deck that includes all the findings and results from your marketing plan. Share this with your team and the executives. Again, this extends your transparency and showcases your great work.

Executive transparency is not all kudos and pats on the back, though. Sometimes you might open a door that allows them to be too involved in your projects, but good leaders will know when to back off. You'll need to learn to mitigate an overly-involved executive and an under-informed one.

Only you, in your specific role, in your unique company, can make the right call. This would be a great topic of discussion with your manager and your team to get a sense of how your company culture perceives the need for executive transparency.

A final little tidbit to help manage up to executives is understanding their SWOTs—please tell me you know what this is! Okay, fine, for good measure, SWOT means Strengths, Opportunities, Weaknesses, and Threats. It's important to get a good grasp of their "third rails,"—i.e. things that are like nails on the chalkboard for them. This way, when you are coming close to doing something that might irk them, you'll know it ahead of time.

If you're working in a smaller company, this is even more important for you. It is better to ask for permission first than forgiveness later in this scenario. Trust me, I have been burned before. You'll find yourself quickly getting to the end of their forgiveness. It will behoove you to try to understand how they like to be managed up to and what their "third rails" are as early in your relationship as you can, and preferably in the interview process, if possible.

I once heard a great anecdote from a previous manager of mine that sweetly sums up the key to being successful at managing in all of these directions. She said to simplify the noise you hear from above and around you—filter out emotions and angst, and focus on the issue at hand—then refresh your understanding of your goals— what they are, why you are meeting the goal, and where you are on the timeline. You must be as prescriptive as possible and give a good business context in everything you do to be an effective marketing starter.

# CHAPTER 6

---

## MAXIMIZE A LIMITED BUDGET

I feel that your ambitions should always exceed the budget.
That no matter what budget you're doing, you should
be dreaming bigger than the budget you have, and then
it's a matter of reigning it into reality.

–Guillermo del Toro
Filmmaker, author, and actor

P ut your entrepreneur hat on for a second and imagine you have a new business idea that is going to change the world, but you have only a few bucks in your pocket to get it off the ground. You have potential investors waiting to see results before they will offer you more funds, so you have to prove your case. You need to show success before you can keep growing. This is what entrepreneurs call "pulling yourself up by your bootstraps."

Over the years, I have learned to stretch budgets quite a bit when launching my startups and in marketing starter roles. I found myself in situations where marketing spend came out of my personal pocket to situations where budgets were well over $1 million. Each budget took profound scrappiness to ensure that the dollars were well spent and close to, but not over, the allotment for the year.

In my channel marketing role with Vendini, my manager, the CRO, was never able to really assign a true budget to my team. Instead, we had to draft on the marketing and product teams while basically bribing engineers to build products we needed. Since we didn't have any real dollar backing, we had to hack our way through our projects by borrowing as many resources as possible from other departments.

During my time with the digital advertising firm, the executive team was extremely cautious of how much time, effort, and money it cost my team to complete projects. With a small $250,000 budget, they severely underestimated nearly everything we did in marketing, especially on the manpower side, which impacted the budget significantly. The good news is that there are ways to navigate all of your budget concerns as a marketing starter with mindfulness of what keeps your management up at night.

## Start on the Cheap

Whether you have a sizable budget or mere pennies to work with, a marketing starter should always look for ways to stretch their funds. Even if you have what feels like an unlimited budget out of the gate, you should start off your new marketing starter role on the cheap.

First off, it's going to take you a minute to understand budget standards for your team, and second, you never know what unexpected expenses might come about in the future.

Marketing tools often make up a sizable part of your budget. For example, Marketo marketing automation licensing costs can start at $20,000 per year, and that's on the low end! Lead sourcing, task organization, social media automation—we all have our wishlist of amazing tools that will often make our jobs so much easier, but if we had our way, it could cost a small fortune. This is why we need to determine what tools we actually need to do our job and do it well. These tools will vary greatly between marketing roles, but there are certainly ones that already stand out in your mind right now. Some costly tools may be crucial to doing your job well. In that case, you must advocate for them and perhaps expand the budget as needed. I talk more about demanding the tools you need in chapter eight.

For now, get the tools you need and table the ones you really don't. Actually, you can level this up by hunting for ones you can get for free. Free versions are a lifesaver. Asana is a great example of this. Their free version is robust, perfect if you're attempting to organize tasks within a small team—plus, their paid version isn't that expensive in case you need to upgrade. A lot of marketing tools follow the "freemium" model. As you're getting started, it would be good to exhaust those tools to their free potential before paying.

> **TIP 28:**
> Freemium is a lifesaver! Get as many free versions of tools as possible, and use the hell out of them until you absolutely need to spring for a paid subscription.

A true skill for you to acquire as a marketing starter is to understand what inexpensive tactics have already driven proven results for your company and try those again. These should be revealed as you're learning the business in the early days, especially if you have upper management marketing support that can shed light on budget-saving techniques. Perhaps someone on your marketing team has a hookup with a direct mail distributor, or someone has a license to a swag platform they can share.

Another great way to find out what budget-saving tactics are at your disposal would be to sit down with your team and brainstorm what your team can do internally to minimize costs.

## Managing and Allocating

A lot of what we do in marketing is trial and error. After all, we didn't coin the term "A/B testing" for nothing. Testing is a big part of marketing, especially starter marketing—I get into how marketing is really a laboratory and not a factory in chapter eight—but guess what can be expensive? Laboratories and testing.

Performing tests on your thoughtful marketing hypotheses costs valuable time and can eat away at chunks of your budget like termites in a 150-year-old house. To combat this, you need to set a certain part of your budget aside for testing new tactics and hypotheses, and leave the rest for investing in effective tactics. I have learned that the best practice here is to allocate about 10 to 20 percent of your budget for testing while using the other 80 to 90 percent of the budget to scale what's already working for you. It really all depends on what you're comfortable with gambling.

In chapter two, I talked about how to steal marketing tactics from competitors as you research them. This can save you big dollars on your marketing budget by employing tested tactics that work for parallel businesses instead of testing new ones. Use what you already know works for competitors and past internal campaigns when allocating your budget.

One of the most frequent questions I have received from hiring managers during interviews or from executives during budget planning is, "How do you know which marketing channels are best to allocate money toward?" The answer I give always defers back to my marketing starter tactic of learning the business.

Typically, I respond by saying that there are proven tactics that work for every business, but that my research into the company's past campaigns, as well as what competitors are doing well, will offer the insight needed to answer that question. I often say that there is no magic eight ball that will give the right answer to that question, and that we really won't know until we investigate. So hire me, and let's investigate together, dammit!

Managing a budget is no easy task, and unless you're obsessed with numbers and dream about manipulating spreadsheets, it's not all that fun either. As marketers, this can often be very distracting from doing our real jobs of marketing the business. However, if we serve in a management role or in a role where we are part of a huge cost center, it is critical.

The trick is to stay organized. One way to do this is to use your charm and become buddies with the folks on the accounting team.

They can help you to better track your expenditures and let you know if something strange has hit your budget lines. You'll see a recurring theme throughout this book of warming up to your co-workers. It's the only way you'll ever get off of Marketing Island!

In one of my director roles, I set up a budget vs. spending balance sheet that tracked my expenses over time and kept a running balance in key categories month-by-month. This way, I knew how much I could allocate to specific items as the year progressed. This turned out to be a perfect tool to share with my manager, as well as the accounting team, so we could keep better track of the marketing expenses that belonged to my specific department. Not to brag, but they loved it!

> **TIP 29:**
> If you're responsible for a budget, create a reverse balance sheet to track how much of your budget you use over time, so you know how best to allocate your funds as the year progresses.

Download the reverse balance sheet
template at themarketingstarter.com.

In that role, I was truly stranded on Marketing Island early on, and I needed every resource I could dig up. I accepted any helping hand available to make my job a bit more streamlined. And, because I got chummy with the accounting team, they offered to send me monthly reports of my expenses, which I could pop into my balance sheet. It made my life so much easier.

## Asking for More

Let's imagine the little company we started at the beginning of the chapter. We have self-funded until now, and the company has grown as far as it can. Now it needs to take on investment. We have been able to achieve great things with the initial money we put into the business from the three Fs: Friends, Family, and Fools. We developed the product and took it to market, built a passionate little team, and established the brand, but now we need a cash infusion to expand. We need to get in front of real investors and get them to buy into our idea.

What would these investors want to hear and see? What would they expect from us to make our case and ultimately cut the check? They always want to know how much, what it's for, and how much the business will grow with the funds. And, of course, they will want to know what their returns will be and when they'll get them.

Much like you would to investors, you need to pitch to your company's money people to increase your budget. For some, it may be with the CFO and executive team. For others, you may be able to get the bump from your direct manager. In either case, marketing starters need to be equipped with convincing plans to prove their case when asking for an increased budget. Here are a few tips:

1. **Set clear goals for the funds.** The number one way to ask for a bigger budget is to set clear business goals for how the money will be used. The goals of the company, especially growth in ROI directly influenced by marketing, should reflect your budget increase. If your revenue targets are growing 10 percent year over year, so should your budget. Company goals are a great initial barometer to determine the amount of your increase.

2. **Get the sales team on your side.** Once you get a good grasp on your growth goals and how much money you'll need, it's also good practice to bounce your new budget off your sales counterparts and get their buy-in. They'll

always love to hear that you're spending money to deliver them more leads. And, if you're doing your job right and all your systems are in place with flawless execution, the only part missing is the money to scale. So, getting your sales team on board gives you more wiggle room if you need it.

3. **Project realistic and optimistic results.** Displaying your projected results based on spending will truly help solidify your case. Don't ask for a million dollars for a specific tactic if you're not sure it's where you should be hedging your bets. Be real! Make sure whomever assigns your funds has a clear understanding of the return on marketing investment. (I'll explain more in chapter eight.)

4. **Don't take more than you need.** Even if it's offered to you, play your "responsible corporate citizen card" and politely refuse so you don't set yourself up for failure. As a career private sector worker, I always make it a goal to stay slightly under budget. It's a growth company after all, and marketing starters treat their budget as if it was their very own.

> **TIP 30:**
> It is in your best interest to use all of your budget, but it's not always the best measurement tool to ask for more. Stay under budget if you can, and put some real metrics together to show your money at work.

On your way into a new role is probably not a good time to ask for more money. Typically, the last quarter of the fiscal year is the time to ask to expand your budget. Either way, you must back up your ask with real numbers.

Never forget this tasty nugget: Marketing should be viewed as a revenue generator and not a cost center! Tie your programs to revenue generation as much as you possibly can—your budget and results will echo this. It is up to you to help yourself and your fellow marketers by backing up your ask with accurate ROI projections. Do yourself and all of us this favor.

Don't worry, you got this!

# CHAPTER 7

---

## GOOD VS. EVIL MARKETING

Don't be afraid to get creative
and experiment with your marketing.

–Mike Volpe
CEO, Lola.com

I cannot tell you how many times I have worked for clients or companies who simply have developed bad marketing practices and continue to replicate them over and over and over. From 10,000 contact spam email campaigns to daily webinars to clip-art presentations, I've seen it all.

Heck, I've made a business helping companies fix their bad marketing. But the real conundrum is when the client believes what they are doing is good marketing, when in fact it is bad.

Try telling your new boss or touchy client that what they're doing sucks. They'll either appreciate your brutal honesty and embrace your ideas, or cut you loose. Both are much better outcomes than being stuck in an evil marketing rut, trust me.

Marketing starters, I'd say, have to deal with these evil practices the most—especially when they find themselves in smaller organizations that may not have been as forward-thinking as they initially anticipated.

A while back I had a short consulting stint with a small financial software company that relied heavily on email as their primary marketing channel. They were a very flat organization with a sole marketer reporting to the CEO—a CEO who had no marketing chops whatsoever, which is totally fine by the way.

He was a fantastic businessman who built two multi-million dollar companies from the ground up, but he was clearly missing that marketing X-factor. When I first met with him before getting hired, he asked me, "What can you tell me about how we should be doing marketing?"

This question came only a few minutes into the conversation, after I had given him a little taste of my marketing background. The fact that this was only his third or fourth question hoisted a big red flag into the air.

I asked him what their current marketing efforts looked like and what channels were working for them, and he repeatedly said, "Email, email, nothing but email." I'm sure you email marketers out there are guessing what my next questions to him were….

Yep, I asked him about the types of email campaigns, where they got their lists, and, of course, how the channel is performing and if they're measuring their ROI. I got a blank stare; he strikingly resembled a little lost puppy looking for a warm new marketing home.

Since it was a small company, I had to offer him some grace. I wasn't out to build a marketing empire at that time. I just wanted to help a scrappy little company get on their marketing feet.

> **TIP 31:**
> Don't be tempted by empire-building because it puts you at risk. Start small and make a clear growth path with the empire as a dream for later on. If you build too quickly, it can be stripped away just as fast as it was put up.

Ultimately, it comes down to determining what business problems we're trying to solve. The tactics should follow. Data and reporting will back up everything you need to do.

### Fix, Tinker, and Rebuild

Like with my financial software client, starter marketers are often dealing with bad or no-marketing situations. Many times, they are either coming in to fix something that's broken or build something that is non-existent—and sometimes they need to do both. The companies in which marketing starters find themselves often need a lot of fixing and and a lot of rebuilding.

In the book *The Powers*, Tony Wessling and Peter van Aartrijk—a terrific branding starter duo by the way—describe how claiming your place in marketing can often feel like a rummage sale. With this insightful metaphor, they describe how brands over time accumulate lots and lots of products, processes, and even identities that can muck up what they stand for and how they are perceived in the marketplace. They advise that all of that junk needs to be sold off to get back to the root of the brand and make way for new, good marketing to flourish.

As a marketing starter, even if we're not in branding, we need to have a rummage sale to clear out all the clutter every time we step into a new role, take on a new client, or start up a new project.

Marketing starters don't just have to build things from scratch—they can also be pioneers by fixing, tinkering with, and rebuilding what is broken in a company's marketing programs.

And by broken, I mean things that are literally broken—like forms not syncing to CRM or extremely disorganized data. Other, less concrete broken things can be antiquated marketing processes, team members who no longer fit, or a negative brand perception in the marketplace.

It's your job as a marketing starter to analyze and understand what's not working so you can fix it, tinker with it, or rebuild it from scratch. Most of this understanding will happen in phase two of the marketing starter approach that I covered in chapter three.

Certainly not every marketing role is going to require a detailed plan that lays out all of your fixes, but you should have a solid idea of how to handle all this and communicate it with your team. Usually when something is broken, everyone is well aware, and fixing it can be another one of those satisfying, low-hanging fruits that is ripe for the picking.

## What Marketing Crisis?

It seems like every time we turn on the news there's a new crisis unfolding that will dramatically change our lives. Whether it's a rapidly-spreading pandemic, political unrest, housing market crash, or the storm of the century bombarding the American coast, everything on the news is so alarming nowadays. They play to our fears to get their clicks, views, and shares.

Now, whether or not you believe those things are impacting your day-to-day life or that you're in immediate danger, I must tell you, these breaking stories are never as bad as they seem in the news. Remember, they're in the business of attracting eyeballs and will do anything to get you to look. Anything. I hope you don't fall for the clickbait when you shouldn't, but you have to appreciate the marketing behind it! They got you to tune in, didn't they? I'd be lying if I said that I didn't click once or twice.

Analogy over.

This may come as a complete shock to you as a professional marketer, but not everything is a damn crisis when it comes to your marketing! The "marketing crisis" is something I have become all too familiar with over the years. It is especially rampant at smaller companies, where little moves in marketing have big impacts across the board.

This is something marketing starters, who champion their initiatives, will undoubtedly feel from time to time—or all the time. Whether it comes from upper management, internal customers, or across departments, the marketing crisis can come from a bunch of directions and become very overwhelming.

Akin to all the crises you hear about in the news, just because someone thinks there's a marketing crisis, doesn't make it so. And sometimes as a starter, you need to learn to mitigate a so-called crisis —or at least put out the flames with your marketing blanket of truth to avoid sheer panic.

This is where your management and interpersonal skills are really put to the test. These skills are especially necessary when managing up, which is the direction from which most of the marketing crises seem to come. If I had a dollar for every super-duper urgent matter that couldn't wait an hour or be taken care of the next business day —well, I'd be rich enough to have someone ghost write this book for me!

> **TIP 32:**
> When addressing a crisis, ask yourself these questions: What is the impact on the business? Is this really a crisis? Who thinks it's a crisis? What is your bandwidth to manage? What resources do you need to mitigate? The answers will help you judge how to tackle the issue.

Crises will vary widely in magnitude based on the role and company, but you can be sure that the higher up you rank, or the smaller your department is, the greater likelihood the crisis will come down on you.

I will never ever tell you to shy away from smaller companies, but finding yourself in a marketing starter role at a larger company will help limit the number of marketing crises that hit you head-on. A cushion between you and whoever ranks above you outside of the marketing department always helps. However, as you are coming to learn in this book, most starter roles are going to be at smaller companies with smaller teams—the perfect intersection for a marketing crisis.

The moral of the story is that a lot of things will be broken and will break in your tenure, but you need to learn to pick your battles and mitigate what is and isn't really a crisis. At the end of the day, things will always point back to your plan. Your marketing plan should account for what is broken (remember the assess and investigate phase in chapter three?). As you're starting to split your time, you'll always want to leave room for more curveball crises that come your way. A good rule is to save 20 percent of your time for last-minute, immediate, have-to-do tasks that will inevitably occur.

TIP 33:
Budget 20 percent of your time/bandwidth for crisis management, last-minute projects, or other curveballs that might come your way, and use the rest on planned initiative.

## It Doesn't Matter What You Sell

Let's get nostalgic for a minute. Remember when you were a kid and you set up a lemonade stand on the sidewalk in front of your house? Well, even if you didn't, you most likely have driven past one or seen one in one of your favorite family sitcoms. The scene usually included a sticky plastic folding table topped with red Solo cups, unevenly cut lemons, and a clear, tall pitcher of sweet and sour nectar to quench the neighbors' thirst on a warm summer day. I had my own lemonade stand every summer when I was a kid.

The little barons of the lemon even had a solid marketing strategy: a poster that read "Lemonade 50 cents" and a vocal kiddo who yelled, "Lemonade! Lemonade! Get your lemonade here!" at every jogger, cyclist, driver, and dog walker who passed by. It was a simple strategy and worked well for the lemonade stand business.

But do you know what? It would have worked just as great if the kids were selling Girl Scout cookies or hosting a car wash for dusty minivans. The sign and that vocal friend would do the trick and drive business. Sure, the time of the year, a perfect high traffic location, and pricing mattered, but the core marketing strategy would be the same.

Just like the kids who could pick between lemonade or a car wash, it doesn't matter what you sell. Plain and simple. It only matters how it's sold and how you reach the most people with your service or product.

I may take a lot of flack for making this bold statement, but whether you are in B2B, B2C, technology, construction, retail, manufacturing, lemonade, or the cookie business, what you're selling doesn't matter.

It just doesn't.

This may sound counter-intuitive to what you have been taught in your marketing career, but life is far more interesting when you flip what you think you know on its head.

Let me clarify what I mean. What your company sells ultimately shouldn't affect your strategy and should never dampen your attitude as a marketing professional.

Marketing starters are versatile and could potentially fit into any organization that sells virtually anything. At the end of the day, the product or service doesn't change how you will approach your marketing strategies—thoroughly, with hustle, and focused on results.

This is something I have always made sure to highlight in my phone interviews with hiring managers. My experiences have mostly been in B2B products and services, but I explain to them that the B2B marketing formula I have used for years would work in their business. Many of those same tactics work in B2C environments as well. But starter marketing isn't about the tactics, it's about the attitude and approach.

It always irks me to my core when I read a B2B tech job posting that requires X+ years of experience within the specified industry, because if they were to hire a truly badass marketer, then it would be more about that marketer's chops than what they know about the industry. I totally get that they are trying to marry marketing experience with industry experience, but in doing so, they are potentially cutting out a load of qualified marketers who, if given the chance to learn, could exceed their marketing expectations.

Have a look at this list of qualifications I pulled out of a job description for a director of marketing operations for a financial services technology company:

- 10–15 years experience in senior operations roles, preferably in Financial Services; last 5+ years orchestrating leading governance and processes
- 7–10 years of relevant leadership experience leading marketing and technology teams larger than 8 people
- Experience must include managing large scale projects and overseeing organizational transformation efforts at a large-scale organization

- Preferred 5+ years of B2B Financial Services industry experience
- Strong people management, including the ability to build a new team and work with diverse skill sets (from technical to strategic resources)
- Strong verbal and written communications
- Technical acumen and understanding of leading marketing tools, platforms, and Agile ways of working
- Ability to manage multiple projects in a dynamic, high-pressure environment
- Cross-functional and multi-phased, complex project management skills
- Strong Knowledge of Project / Program management
- Working knowledge of Marketing technologies, especially tools tied to governance, process automation, marketing automation, and resource management

What a mouthful! I wish I was making this up, but I copied this directly from a job board! Seriously, who checks all those boxes? I want to meet the person who does and give them an award.

Clearly, marketing operations roles like the one above are pretty intensive, but I can tell you this: I could do this role and kick ass at it if given the chance. Not because I have stellar operations skills, or the ridiculous amount of financial services experience they require, but because I can learn the nuances of the industry and the processes and systems they require. Plus, I'm a scrappy and tenacious marketing starter, dammit!

But are *they* willing to take the chance? Can I convince *them* too?

To be clear, marketing operations isn't my schtick, so I'd pass on this one, but the point is that they would most likely pass on me because of how important financial services experience is to them.

As I mentioned earlier in the book, I have worked in print media, digital media, ticketing, advertising, corporate real estate, telecommunications, events, security, and travel. It never mattered what they sold, because I had the ability to apply kickass marketing tactics while learning the industry at the same time. Sure, I didn't know all the industry acronyms or how diversified the competitive landscape was at the start, but those things can be learned quickly by learning the business—which is a callback to chapter two.

**TIP 34:**

Even though it doesn't matter what you sell, it's important to understand the product and how it's sold. Do your due diligence when you land the job at your new company and get up to speed on what they sell.

I'm just going to say it: The requirement for a multitude of years of industry experience is straight bullshit. If you see a job that asks for this, skip it, because they don't get the concept of being a starter. They're looking for insiders who are gonna keep the status quo churning along.

They are not looking for a disruptor, an outsider with new ideas. I get how having industry experience is good, but it shouldn't be a deal-breaker, and it shouldn't be required with an emphasis on a certain number of years. Industries and what they sell can be learned much faster than any skill you have acquired while building your starter background. Keep starting and keep searching for the company that believes in you as a starter.

## Labs Are Greater than Factories

What do you think of when you imagine a factory? Are you picturing Lucille Ball in that infamous episode of *I Love Lucy* where she couldn't keep up with the chocolates coming down the conveyor belt, so she started to eat them and hide them in her pockets until it all overflowed? Or perhaps you think of the great Ford assembly line with workers at different stations fashioning their part of an automobile as it inches its way forward.

Now, what comes to mind when you imagine a laboratory? Do you see would-be chemists wearing white cloaks and eye goggles carefully examining beakers filled with mysterious liquids resting on stainless steel countertops? As you picture a factory and a lab, I hope you notice one clear difference between the two. Factories assemble and laboratories create.

"Labs are greater than factories" is an amazing quote I heard when attending the HOW Marketing Live conference a few years back. Since marketing starters are part scientists, we should all appreciate this mantra. We think differently, we experiment, and we know when to mix things up.

Oftentimes, marketers feel the heat from their internal customers to churn and burn on their marketing tasks. Create ten blog posts a month, do a ton of customer case studies, and share every waking moment in the company on social media. While this volume can seem like a great KPI, it most certainly is not. In fact, it's a marketing factory approach.

I always imagine a T-shirt factory with all its machinery, conveyor belts, presses, and shelves of colorful fabric paint. A factory with raw materials on one end and beautifully finished graphic tees spitting out the other. From the moment the whistle blows at 8:00 a.m, the place is buzzing with the sole purpose of making as many T-shirts as it possibly can by the time the day is over. Sure, this factory can create some variety in its shirts—i.e. color and size—but the second a custom job is required, the factory needs to reconfigure its entire process or employ specialists with new equipment to get the job done. You'd like a unique blend tie-dyed T-shirt with your logo filled in with sequins—though I'm not sure why you would. They can do it, but it's going to take some time and extra resources they don't normally have.

Marketing's products cannot be built in a factory. Marketing's KPI is not how much it can produce, but how effective it is. To be effective, marketing cannot exist in a factory. It must be made in a laboratory. Marketers are not in the quantity game; rather, they're in the quality game, and quality simply does not come from a factory. Marketing is more of a science than an industry. Marketers are constantly performing experiments and testing outcomes to see what tactics will work best, and there's simply no room for experiments in factories.

A great example of a marketing factory being pushed on me was when I was working for a smaller company. The CEO was very keen on webinars—a little too keen. The company had seen previous success in driving MQLs from engaged webinar audiences, and he believed that expanding the company's webinar presence would drive more business. He was right. Well, partially.

What I came to discover was that he wanted to go far beyond industry norms and the capabilities of my team to execute webinars effectively. He believed that more webinars equaled more leads, despite my desperate attempts to convince him that they would dramatically lose effectiveness if we continued to market them at volume to our audience over and over. Alas, my pleas fell on deaf ears. I was overruled and forced to create a webinar marketing factory with my team.

We ended up hosting five live webinars per week, one to each of our key industries. These took my marketing team hours to organize and promote, as well as to coordinate with the sales team who had to present them. In a perfect world, this strategy would be great for a company that had an immense prospect list and the internal bandwidth to perform at this rate, but as a small company, we just weren't there yet. We were literally churning and burning and quickly saw success metrics of the webinars drop off a very steep cliff. A marketing lead experiment of one to two webinars carrying content to key segments would have been much more effective, but our lab was overruled with a factory mentality.

I once heard a quote from an unknown marketer that said, "Behind every piece of bad content is an executive who asked for it." Boy, were they ever right!

Sometimes CEOs and other executive leaders who have a taste for marketing will take an unprovoked interest in your lab. They'll tinker and try their damndest to turn it into a factory. You must use caution and remain respectful while balancing their requests with what really needs to be done to create a successful marketing program.

Never allow your laboratory to turn into a cold, dark, soot-filled factory. Laboratories are built on finesse, testing, and experimentation, but also back up performance with experience and skill. Stand firm in your belief of running your marketing programs like a laboratory, and be clear in your expectations to employees and management so they understand and respect your marketing lab coat.

## Done Is Better than Perfect

This motto is just too damn good not to repeat: Done is better than perfect.

I simply cannot express how much this simple little mantra means to marketers—especially marketing starters. The first time I heard this phrase I was in a one-on-one meeting with my sales leader at the digital advertising company where I worked. He expressed that in an effort to move quickly, measure success, and make change, projects needed to get done and shipped with haste. He strongly believed that striving for perfect would cripple our efforts to drive the business forward. Simply put, perfection never gets done.

I heard him say this many times to his team and in meetings with our executive team. I took this to heart because it was something that fit right into the mentality of my marketing starter worldview. I simply didn't have the bandwidth for perfect, but better was always just around the corner.

Think about it: We're human, and we are far from perfect, so there's no way in hell that the programs and projects that we create can ever be. We'll never reach the perfect target audience. We'll never get our marketing automation and sales CRM working 100 percent correctly. The copy on our website will never quite resonate and increase page session duration the way we hope it will. If we strive for perfect, we'll simply never see our creations come to life and never be able to assess them. Honestly, why even start if you're aiming for perfect?

Seth Godin—author, AMA Marketing Hall of Fame inductee, and all-around super marketer—has a very insightful opinion on perfection. He believes that perfection is tyranny and that it asserts that we have done the absolute best we can achieve. The concept of perfection handicaps marketers by forbidding us to try any harder.

Think about the previous section. There is no perfect in a laboratory, only trial after trial until you get close enough. And most of the time close enough will work just fine. Do I think this book is perfect? Hell no! It certainly is good enough, though, and most importantly, it's done. It's in your hands or on your eBook. I can surely tell you that I'll learn from this writing experience and make the next one even better.

**TIP 35:**
Remove perfect from your vocabulary. Do it right now! A marketing starter has no room for perfect. We must churn and burn, build and measure. Always be striving for better, not perfect.

Like *close enough,* Seth Godin said that there is magic in *good enough.* Good enough gives us the opportunity to learn from mistakes and embrace the ultimate probability of better. It enables us to better serve our customers and build trust.

# CHAPTER 8

---

## STARTER ROMI

We tend to overvalue the things we can measure
and undervalue the things we cannot."

–John Hayes
Author of *The Theory and Practice of Change Management*

As business-minded people, we are all too familiar with the
acronym ROI, which stands for return on investment. In fact,
it might be the most overused term in the business dictionary. What
was new to me in my early days as a marketing starter was the term
ROMI, or return on marketing investment. I first heard this term
from a speaker at a marketing conference, who was delineating the
difference in total company investment and activity (which leads to
ROI), and the marketing department investment and activity (which
leads to ROMI).

I found this comparison striking because, at that time, I was
solely concerned about total ROI for my company. Of course, I
tracked marketing's influence, but never considered the specific
investment return that could be attributed to the marketing department directly. I found this novel idea enlightening.

I took this learning and was able to develop strategies that led to
better tracking of marketing investment and the outcomes that
marketing was specifically able to generate. These outcomes are what
dramatically changed my view on marketing KPIs. Marketing can

now achieve their KPIs while putting goals back on internal stake-holders to ensure marketing investment in the future. Marketing starters should one hundred percent care about the company's ROI and how they fit into that wheel, but need to stay focused on the ROMI for their specific programs.

An example that immediately comes to mind is when my team managed all conference appearances for my company. Before I arrived to restart marketing, sales drove conference sponsorships and would pick which conferences to attend by employing a low-grade vetting process. This, paired with poor tracking techniques, led the company to never gain a real understanding of what and how much business came out of these pricey conferences.

When I came into the company, I understood how much marketing invested in planning to attend these conferences. It took tons of manpower and accounted for nearly a third of the department's overall budget. Measuring the ROMI for each conference was an immediate need and something I wanted to be sure to have a firm grasp on.

The first thing I set in place was the ability to track an opportunity pipeline to ultimately win business from specific conferences. As I built this, I gave sales one simple rule: if they don't win any business from a specific event, then we will not attend or sponsor it the next year. Once I created that mandate and got buy-in from the sales director, it created a sense of urgency for sales reps to work their post-conference leads, close deals, and log them properly into the CRM.

A lot of investment went into conference planning, and not just from marketing. Conference campaigns include marketing time and dollars, sales time and dollars, and even, at times, executive time and dollars. With all those cost-centers involved in conferences, I asked our accounting team to provide a detailed report of all expenses related to the conference from all the parties involved.

> **TIP 36:**
> As you're investigating your marketing infrastructure, learn how you can keep track of marketing ROMI with the tools you have at your disposal.

Once I received the report, we took that total number and put it into the CRM campaign as total cost, which was able to get us the total, true ROI. We calculated the ROMI based on marketing's spend and time invested, and that included supporting campaigns as advertisements run during the conference. Boom, we had our solution.

Whether tangible or abstract, it's imperative for marketing starters to discover ways to calculate their ROMI with tangible metrics like dollars and hours.

**Beware of Vanity Metrics**

Another great lesson learned at a conference was the concept of vanity metrics. Vanity metrics are those stats that companies, and more specifically marketing departments, love to flaunt, but that don't mean a whole lot in the real world. They are shiny objects that are fun to talk about, but do not drive business in a real way. It's kind of like a dog that's all bark and no bite.

Vanity metrics are typically known as things like impressions, likes, followers, shares, comments, views, bounce rates, etc. You can read article after article about vanity metrics and how much of a time suck they can be, but basically these are numbers that rarely correlate to actual business being won.

To continue with my conference example, it could be business cards collected, booth traffic, session attendance, or badges scanned. While they all show myriad activities, which do show interest, they don't show any tangible results and, therefore, are hard to tie directly to ROI or CLTV (a.k.a. Customer Lifetime Value).

Just because a metric is a vanity doesn't mean it has no value. There are plenty of brands and influencers who make serious money based on their subscriber numbers alone. But you need to think: Is that the business model you are operating in? Probably not.

Vanity metrics do help gauge brand equity and popularity, but should not be your primary measurement of success, especially in B2B marketing. Imagine reporting to your executive team week after week how many Instagram followers you get as your primary metric of success when you're supposed to be driving leads to sales. Now imagine them laughing you right out of the room!

> **TIP 37:**
> People who pretend to know about marketing, or marketing posers, care a lot about vanity metrics. Be their guide and point them toward the right measurements.

There are two reasons you may want to focus on vanity metrics: if your company is somehow tied intimately to social media—for example, if your brand relies on influencers for sales—or your CEO just really cares about them. My advice is to expand beyond those metrics to see what can be made actionable from them. Did those shares turn into purchases? Did that email bounce rate drop significantly because you cleaned up the contact database?

I'm not saying you should completely disregard vanity metrics; rather, don't make them your north star or crowning achievement of your marketing programs—unless you're a social media manager and those are your main KPIs, then keep at it!

## Demand the Right Tools

The key to properly tracking ROMI is—surprise, surprise—implementing the right processes and tools. If your company is super ROI focused, which hopefully everyone is, then they will have no problem supporting you with the tools you need to properly track and measure.

I mentioned assessing the tools you really need in chapter six, and the ones which help you drive and measure ROMI should be high on that priority list. Could you imagine tracking your website traffic growth without a tool like Google Analytics? How about deducing top lead sources without a marketing automation tool like Marketo? If a primary goal of your company is to get a better grasp on measurable results, and they don't have the tool kits to measure or report, then you need to demand them. If they don't comply, then run!

> **TIP 38:**
> Compare your company's current list of marketing tools against your wishlist, then request the ones you need to do your job the right way.

Demand is a strong word, but I use it because you need the right tools to do your job well and efficiently, and you need the ones you know how to use. Could you imagine if a plumber were given the toolbox of a hairstylist? Sure, maybe the plumber could use the scissors to trim plumber's tape, but how could she properly install a new sink without a pipe wrench?

You need to have the right tools for the job, and you need to make the case for them with your higher-ups.

Let's be real: Some of these tools can be pretty darn expensive, and with marketing's already horrible reputation as a cost center, this can certainly work against you. But it's your responsibility to make the case for that expensive new tool, its benefit, and its ultimate ROI for the company. Do your homework and prepare a tight pitch before you go asking for $30,000 for a new CRM and marketing automation tool. And don't forget chapter six: Be modest with your budget, dammit!

# CHAPTER 9

---

## EMBRACE THE VOLATILITY

Ever tried. Ever failed. No matter.
Try Again. Fail again. Fail better.

–Samuel Beckett
Novelist and playwright

M arketing starters must learn to embrace the volatility of company structure, which is much, much easier said than done. Marking starters will often find themselves in roles at small to mid-sized companies, which can and will experience many ups and downs in very short spans of time. Picture a windy, choppy day in a small harbor with little boats bobbing up and down as the waves roll in.

The calmer waters of large enterprise companies may offer marketing starter roles as well, but the bigger they get, the fewer they will have. Big enterprises typically have very clearly defined marketing role swim lanes that don't require the broad skill sets of marketing starters. You can easily pick this up when looking at a job description of a small company versus a big one.

Remember that qualifications list I mentioned for the director of marketing operations position for a financial services company from chapter seven? Flip back there real quick to have a look before moving on.

Read it? Okay, great. Now look at this description for a director of marketing at a smaller startup:

- 8–10 years of marketing experience, SaaS and high-growth marketing experience preferred
- 2–5 years of management experience
- Track record of building marketing campaigns and strategies that result in product adoption and/or revenue
- Experience planning, creating, executing, and measuring multi-channel marketing campaigns
- Strong project management and organizational skills, with the ability to juggle multiple projects while still working effectively
- Can set priorities, meet deadlines, and work independently
- Pays close attention to detail and has strong writing and editing skills
- Ability to juggle multiple priorities and choose the right ones
- Is curious by nature and has a growth mindset

Now I know these aren't apples to apples, but as you read them both you can certainly feel that the larger company wants something —or, should I say, someone—super specific, whereas the smaller company is looking for someone more broad, certainly more starter-minded.

SMBs that are growing rapidly and are nimble are much more likely to need marketers who can come in and build the necessary processes they need from scratch and scale them quickly. The trick here is to be ready and embrace the volatility of the company that will come into your little harbor. And much like startup founders, marketing starters need to be ready to embrace change and manage the crises of these demanding roles.

## Fail as Fast as Possible

For most of us, our paths to success are built on long episodes of trial and error, or failure, to be more truthful. Take James Dyson for example—you know, the vacuum guy. Dyson is a shining beacon of how failure can turn into success. Fifteen years and more than 5,000 failed prototypes after he began, he finally succeeded in creating the world's first bagless vacuum cleaner. On top of all that, he became nearly bankrupt and received rejection after rejection before he finally landed a licensing agreement. Today, Dyson is one of the bestselling (and most expensive) vacuum cleaners worldwide.

> **TIP 39:**
> Failure is scary, but you must embrace it. Sure, you may blow up the lab a few times, but think of all the ways you'll learn how not to blow it up in the future.

Failure was something Dyson actually thrived in. He once said, "You can never learn from success." He sounds like a true starter if I ever heard one.

How many times do you attempt something new before giving up? Whether it's a new sport, hobby, or invention of your own? I bet you've not yet hit 5,000 prototypes, though. Dyson knew he would eventually perfect his bagless vacuum technology. He knew he would fail—although maybe he didn't predict 5,000 times—but he knew. He also knew that no matter the odds (in this case, one in 5,000), he must keep trying, and eventually, he was successful. Case in point: Never give up.

By the way, the first Dyson vacuum wasn't perfect by any means, but he sure got it done!

From Samuel Beckett's quote at the beginning of the chapter, I take "fail better" to mean failing fast and understanding what led to that failure in the first place. Great thinkers and innovators are not perfect; they fail all the time. It's how they handle their failures and learn from them that makes them great. In my entrepreneurship lessons, I was taught to prepare for failure. I also learned the best strategy of all: *When* you fail you should fail fast, take the learnings, then try again.

That's exactly what Dyson did. He failed 5,000 times, but each time he quickly incorporated what he learned and tried again until he succeeded.

### Ride the Wave

One tool you're going to need close by your side on Marketing Island is a surfboard. There will be a lot of waves to ride as you start to venture out.

As I mentioned earlier, more often than not, marketing starters find themselves in roles with SMBs. And SMBs have lots of growing pains—from being pre-revenue to fumbled acquisitions to bad hiring practices to security breaches to company-wide layoffs. I've literally seen and been through it all.

Experiencing growing pains like these are a big part of working for growth companies and should be something you're prepared for. In fact, this is something I have spoken at conferences about—the theme being "how to grow with a growth company." Marketing starters should be well-versed in how these ebbs and flows of growth companies affect their jobs. Of course, there are two vastly different sides to the coin of the growing pain.

The rapid growth of these nimble companies is what has created the opening for marketing starters to land and start building. The strong desire of the companies to look for a marketing stater itself is an excellent barometer for the health and culture of the company.

Expanding marketing departments and investing in not-so-typical marketing personnel show that the company is forward-thinking and investing in their future. If a prospective company is doing this, marketing starters should be excited.

I went on and on about my marketing starter stories in chapter three, with the many ups and downs. If you're in need of a refresher, head back there.

Quite possibly the shortest wave I ever rode as a marketing starter was during my time at Dialpad. I was beyond excited to work for a larger growth tech company with a fancy open office, free healthcare, and catered lunches. But even more valuable to me was the role, which was chock-full of starter responsibilities aligned tightly with a group that drove 30 percent of the pipeline and saw extreme growth. But what happened after being there for only nine months?

I was laid off along with about sixty others across nearly every department (sans engineering, of course). Nine frickin' months. That was barely enough time to get past Phase 1 of my Three-Phase approach, and certainly not enough time to operate at a more strategic level or hire the support team that was promised to me.

Here's the thing: As bitter as I may sound, it's not their fault. It's not my boss's fault, nor the CMO's. Heck, I can't even blame the CEO that much, or even the board. I once again was a victim of the crappy circumstances that came with being considered part of the fat that needed to be cut.

It happens.

I'm not gonna cry about it, but it only helps to remind me that I always need to be prepared to ride the wave and roll with the ups and downs of a rapidly changing growth company.

During the post-Dialpad season, I realized it was the third year in a row that I was out of work during Q4, all in a bustling economy with the lowest unemployment rate since the 1960s.

I joked with my wife, who was always jealous of the ridiculous perks of a tech gig, that no matter how great those perks may seem, she always had a job in her industry. Consistency in her career has always existed. You don't usually hear about mass layoffs in healthcare.

But hey, that's dentistry for you. Tech is just that way. Marketing is just that way. And you have to be prepared for it.

On the flip side of the coin, however, is a much different perspective and one that marketing starters should also be prepared for: explosive growth. Sometimes companies grow so fast you'll feel like your head is spinning during your entire tenure. You need to be able to grow alongside your hyper-growth company.

That stupid catchphrase, "Throw you in the deep end," is what I'm talking about here, except that the deep end keeps getting deeper and you keep getting farther from the edge. You better be a damn good swimmer!

Marketing starters, by trait, are good swimmers, but you must have the gumption to build the boat while treading water or at least ask someone to throw you a life ring so you can stay afloat. Resourcefulness will always get you out of these jams, even if it means moving on to the next starter role.

Layoffs and IPOs are obviously extreme cases in which you need to ride the wave. However, the waves flow very much in between those extremes.

My time at Vendini was a real wave to ride. The company was growing like crazy and needed a marketing starter to help out. It was the perfect fit for me. I was hire number eighty-something, and the company nearly doubled in size in the time I was there. They also reached the $20 million mark and raised their first-ever round of funding.

Vendini acquired two companies, both of which had consumer-facing applications that fell under my purview. To adapt, I quickly ramped up my staff and set all the plans to scale my programs. But, shortly after my three-year mark, I, along with about 40 other staffers, were laid off because of slowing revenue growth. This was heartbreaking, of course, but not something new.

I had been through the layoff game before and it totally sucked, but I knew I would come out the other side. The Vendini story didn't stop there. They were able to lean up and refocus their efforts, and not long after I was gone, they were acquired by a larger ticketing software company.

My story there was over by that time, but I couldn't help but think of how the future looked to the other marketing starters who were there from the beginning through the acquisition. What a ride.

When I was with the advertising company, their wave came in the form of trust. I was promised a generous line of trust in my expertise when I first landed, but it turns out that upper management had a hard time stepping aside to let the leaders below them take the helm.

And that's okay. It happens a lot at smaller companies, but that lack of trust in my expertise ultimately led to my decision to leave the company to pursue something where I could have full autonomy.

> **TIP 40:**
> Job security isn't real. Never assume that you're immune to layoffs or losing your job. This will keep you humble in your work and more composed when it happens. Ride the wave.

The point here is that marketing starters should be prepared for ups and downs, especially if they work in tech. Company outlooks change just as fast as the products themselves.

The good thing is that no matter what happens while you're riding the marketing starter career wave, there is one major benefit you can fall back on: You don't have to beg for your old job back. There's always another marketing starter job and a progressive company where you can fit right in.

# CHAPTER 10

---

## SET YOURSELF UP FOR SUCCESS

Success doesn't come to you... you go to it.

–Marva Collins
American educator

The trick behind being a good marketing starter—the point I am trying to get across in this book—is to set yourself up for success. Your processes and documentation of those processes are the key to your success, and, just as important, the success of your programs.

**Write It Down**

This may sound ridiculously obvious, but so many of us forget to do this one trivial, yet vital thing: Write it down. It's certainly true that the students who excel in class take the best notes and have written plans.

In chapter two, I talked about the assessment phase (Phase 1), in which you dig into current marketing operations of your new job. This phase is where you gather all the current written processes and get them organized into one single repository. This is step one of being successful. Step two is to properly document all your new processes and get those organized into the fold as well.

While this careful documentation may not be the best form of job insurance, it does help you be an outstanding corporate citizen. It's also helpful in the extreme case that you get hit by a bus on your way to the office and your employees need to take over in your stead. Sorry to be so grim! I suppose a better example would be if you happen to abruptly leave the company.

> **TIP 41:**
>
> In early sync-ups with your employees, ask them what processes and protocols would be dead in the water if they were to get hit by a bus. Then, have them write down how to operate them!

An excellent exercise is to create process documents when you are on your way out of a company to leave behind for your reports, management, and possible replacement. Not only will this humble you and help your colleagues, it will help sharpen your writing skills for when you need to document your systems in your new marketing starter role.

Clearly, this is much easier to do when the departure is amicable. Just some food for thought.

Getting processes and how-tos down on paper will certainly grow your favorability with executives, because it shows them you have put careful thought into how you do your work. It also gives them transparency into how your systems work. I'm sure they'll never end up sitting down to read them, but there may be an off chance they have hours to spend analyzing your marketing jargon.

Your marketing plans and campaign docs should be chock-full of these processes in link-offs or addendums. And just like your marketing plan, your processes change frequently, and your documentation should reflect that.

A good marketing starter should be conscious of this and make sure to set time aside at least every six months, depending on how fast your marketing cycle is, to review the documents and make necessary updates. You're not alone in this, though. Be sure to coach your team to help you with reviewing and updating documentation.

## Communicate Your Value

Communication is the basis of all good marketing. Marketers on all levels and across all specialties rely on good communication. It's a good thing we all went to school and have made a career out of being fantastic communicators! Well, maybe some of us aren't communication pros, but we need to learn to advocate for ourselves and sometimes even fight for our value. Marketing starters are no exception.

More often than not, the start of our endeavors takes much longer than expected and tends to drag on. We go off plan and miss deadlines. Budgets get blown and systems break down, which can seriously test the patience and understanding of management, counterparts, and internal customers right out of the gate. This may come as a shock to some of you, but people may not be as empathetic in the workplace as you'd hope, especially if revenue is on the line.

> **TIP 42:**
> Take advantage of your company's internal communication channels—whether it's an online chat room, internal emails, or company-wide meetings—to share your marketing wins. Take advantage of every opportunity to share how marketing is helping your team.

Expectations for ourselves may not always match the expectations that others have for us. So the onus is on marketing starters to make it clear that their objectives are being achieved, no matter how small. We must show that we are moving the needle constantly or that we are offering some sort of intrinsic value as we build our marketing superstructures.

A phrase that I live by in both my personal and professional life is "fortune favors the bold." This means that good fortunes come to those who take chances and live with gumption. Marketing starters should tattoo this on their hearts and communicate their value loudly and proudly, while staying humble and avoiding cockiness.

Make sure people know what you're doing, and don't appear idle in your dark marketing corner of the office.

One of the most important reasons for communicating your value is to achieve executive buy-in. Hopefully they have already bought into your prowess as a marketing starter—otherwise you wouldn't be there, but you must do everything you can to squash the seeds of doubt and continue to keep them in your corner by communicating your value.

It's fine if it's taking you a bit longer than expected and that your budget is off track—just make sure you help your colleagues understand why and keep them sold on your plan.

## Always Keep Track

I once impressed my manager with a budget for my team that included a running monthly balance under each major expense section. I know this sounds a bit nerdy and paltry, but the balance line for each major expenditure section helped me to be proactive and keep tabs on how much cash I had left in my budget, my burn rate, and the running total for the year.

At the risk of bragging, it was pretty cool. I'm sure I wasn't the first marketer to ever think to do that, but I had never seen it before, so I got bold and made my own. My manager loved it so much that she shared the template with her other reports to follow the same model.

I wanted to set myself up for success by better managing my budget and trying to use most of it, with measures to show the specifics, which I knew would make it easier to ask for more money the next year. It also gave my manager the inside look she needed to keep track of her overall department budget.

I also shared this document with the accounting team to help me make sure the expenses matched their accounts payable records. Trust me, I am not a numbers guy, but I do love a well-organized spreadsheet. Especially when it helps to avoid big questions and do my job a little better.

> **TIP 43:**
>
> Spreadsheets are your friend. Create spreadsheets with multiple tabs to track your budget, project metrics, and KPIs. Share it with your manager for easy access.

Download the sample marketing budget
template at themarketingstarter.com.

Reports like the one I made for my budget are super easy to make, don't take that much time, and are a great way for you to keep track of your metrics.

Maybe you don't do email marketing because that's handled by your marketing operations team. They send emails on your behalf through Hubspot or some other marketing automation tool, which is fantastic, but where is the reporting? They have it under lock and key, or at least login credentials. What if you need to run a report?

This is one of the fantastic processes to create when you're first building out your program—something akin to having the marketing operations team send you a performance report after each email blast.

Honestly, it's kind of their job to do this. Ask for the number of emails sent, bounced, and opened, as well as stats for unsubscribes and clicks. List growth is nice too. I promise I'm not going to go down the email marketing rabbit hole. I just want to illustrate how you can keep track of what's happening in your marketing starter bubble.

The purpose of keeping track is to be more successful by being accountable to your internal customers, managing your performance over time, and, of course, advocating for yourself. If I can go back to the previous section for a second: How can you possibly communicate your value when you have no idea what that value is because you didn't keep track?!

This is exactly why your processes should be documented, and you must—I demand it—keep track of your metrics and KPIs over time. Getting distracted or being lazy will be the crutch here. Take a few seconds to set up tracking mechanisms or whatever you need to get that data humming!

It's a bit of legwork in the beginning, but trust me, once it's built, your report tracking will pay off.

# CHAPTER 11

---

## THE MARKETING STARTER CURSE

But it's our curse and our blessing to remember
the past and to know there's a future.

–Susan Beth Pfeffer
Author

This chapter is a word of caution to marketing starters who live from build to build, who either don't have the opportunity or don't have desire to see the results of those builds.

You know who you are, you little marketing thrill-seeker, you!

While having the skill set to plan and build great marketing processes is highly valuable, it can be tough to convey the ultimate success of your work when you're not there long enough to see your vision become a reality. This is especially true when hunting for new career opportunities.

If you search for "marketing resume tips" or survey recruiters, they suggest proudly displaying your KPIs. Prospective employers will want to see the tangible success you achieved, along with the duties performed in your current and past roles, which are equally, if not more, important. Prospective employers want to see clear metrics associated with your role, metrics that can be difficult to convey if you're a marketing starter.

These metrics could be increases in MQLs, increases in CLTV, decreases in CAC, email list growth, website traffic, and attributed revenue, just to name a few. If you have worked in multiple marketing starter roles, where most of your responsibility has been focused on planning, organization, and building, it may be difficult to come up with these metrics.

In many of my roles, I've had to determine how building the groundwork for successful marketing alone was a great KPI.

This is akin to a serial entrepreneur who has launched multiple companies (which I have also been) but has never seen any of them take the ride on the infamous hockey-stick of growth.

Serial entrepreneurs typically jump from idea to idea and build amazing products, but leave before the business matures. Do these startup founders have no accomplishments to share? Has their hard work amounted to nothing? Of course not! There is always a story to be told that came out of the brilliance, hard work, and determination of creating these companies. The same holds true for marketing starters and the lessons we learn from our own experiences.

## Create Sticky KPIs

As you're getting started, it is important to curate KPIs that matter most to your role as a marketing starter. Since marketing supports sales first and foremost, a KPI for every marketing role should obviously be leads and revenue. However, since marketing tasks and specialties are so vast, it can be difficult to attribute efforts directly to leads.

Take branding for example. Try to think of a measurable way in which releasing a new company logo or re-tooling a tag line directly impacts sales. Pretty difficult, isn't it?

If your role is not directly tied to revenue production, it can be almost impossible to determine how your actions directly impacted revenue. This is why you must create and monitor KPIs that are specific to your role.

Get creative with your goals. Maybe your KPI was to complete the aforementioned branding exercise in a certain amount of time or implement a new marketing automation tool that's rolled out to the entire marketing team.

You should be able to convey your KPIs clearly when talking to prospective employers. Share accomplishments like, "During the first six months in my role, I built a new brand strategy and then rebuilt the website from scratch with updated messaging to align with that strategy." The tangible benefit was the short amount of time it took you to do a daunting task like building a new website and crafting brand messaging. Explain how your role was unique, and own it!

> **TIP 44:**
> Determine how you can apply tangible KPIs to your tasks. Write them down and track them over time. Those metrics will look great on your resumé.

Let's use the role of email marketing starter as an example.

Imagine your company has a basic Mailchimp account and has been using it to send periodic prospecting emails in an irregular cadence. The lists are unorganized and outdated. The templates are stale and off-brand. Even the footer shows the wrong phone number. The email marketing program needs a complete overhaul.

Sure, you can easily look at how you improved open and click-through rates, list sizes, and growth, but there is so much more to the project than just that. In this example, the KPIs would include: updated email templates to match the brand, organized and cleaned lists, and created a regular blast schedule for newsletters and customer emails. Plus, it was all done within 60 days.

Clearly the project could go so much deeper, but you can see how being able to convey starter KPIs is important, especially if your next employer is looking for someone to overhaul their email marketing or build it from scratch.

Every marketing role has a set of sticky KPIs that you can point to when your management team comes calling or when you interview with recruiters. You just need to do a little soul searching to find which ones best align with what you do—and it's okay if they are not all numbers!

## Stay Beyond the Start

If you're a true starter at heart, no matter what you do, you'll have an innate desire to keep starting over and over. And who can blame you? It's simply in your nature. However, having this kind of "churn and burn" mentality may not be best if you're trying to land a new job.

It can work great for consultants who want to solely focus on helping companies get started, but potential employers will want you to stay long term.

This is why I urge everyone, not just marketing starters, to stay a year or two (at minimum) at any given job to allow for true, tangible results to trickle in. In the uber distracting world in which we live today, we often have unrealistic expectations that we'll be able to see tangible results in a short time, but reality says much different. I'm talking to you, Gen Z! Obviously, this depends greatly on the role, but starters have a bit more of a challenge.

A salesperson could hit the ground running and crush their quarterly goals immediately upon starting a new position, especially if they have familiarity with the market and the product. A brilliant software engineer can apply her masterful coding skills and fix major bugs within weeks on the new job.

But imagine if either of these people were also tasked with being starters in their departments. What if they not only had to make sales and fix software bugs, but they also had to build the processes and manage the teams that kept their department running? It would be unimaginable for them to form strong results in such a short time, even if they did everything right.

It is the same for marketing starters, primarily because marketing has so many moving parts and is highly collaborative with other departments. That's why I believe it's important to stay past the building phase to see what your marketing creation can and will become.

In fact, your true success is not just measured by what or how much you've built, but by how well it works. Your newly completed, shiny marketing machine should work brilliantly and efficiently. It should be able to churn out measurable results like none other. If it doesn't, then you're not done building.

To go back to the James Dyson example from earlier, it took him more than 5,000 tries to get his vacuum design to work, but that was just version one. From there, he tweaked his design to allow for more suction, and he replaced standard wheels with their famously designed roller ball.

Dyson didn't stop at version one and say, "Well, it's time to throw in the towel on this vacuum thing and go start something else." He saw his creation through, ensuring it was one of high quality and would consistently perform when replicated. You should do the same with your marketing creations. Go beyond the build to see all your hard work come to fruition and bring in tangible results —results you can print on a plaque and frame in your office, or at least add as a line item on your resumé.

## Position Yourself

Now it's time to get a little meta. You need to figure out how to best position yourself and how to tell a great story around what you have accomplished as a marketing starter. You should already be great at positioning, because, heck, you're a professional marketer. Positioning is one of the most important activities we do as marketers. So, in line with crafting your sticky KPIs, you should also learn how to position yourself.

Whether proving your case to your colleagues, boss, or prospective employers, having your positioning nailed down is a must-do. When I say "positioning," I mean an explanation or story about your marketing starter tasks. This means clearly conveying why your KPIs are what they are and how you performed your tasks.

> **TIP 45:**
> Develop your positioning statement. Keep it simple, relatable, and honest. It should reflect who you are professionally while offering a unique slant.

The concept for this book was birthed out of my attempts to position myself as a professional. When I was on calls with recruiters and hiring managers for possible job opportunities, I explained my wide skill set, variety of roles, and even tenure brevity by describing my marketing starter mindset and how I fit into companies looking to build things.

And you know what, they bought it! And they should have, because it was true, and because it was positioning they could understand and relate to.

I loved my personal positioning as a marketing starter so much that I made it part of my Linkedin headline and then decided to write a book about it.

Many other professionals also include intriguing headlines that position themselves clearly and concisely. Here are some of my favorites (names lovingly changed by me):

- Tayla W. - Personal & branding consultant, TEDx Speaker, and award-winning marketing scholar
- Pinaki S. - Helping founders launch startups | Enabling Creative Ideas | Product to Market | Advisor | Storyteller
- Deborah A. - Helping speakers finish their books | Book Coaching Program | Book Creation eLearning | Ghostwriter | Editor
- Ahmed M. - Marketing Coach | I help consultants go from "best-kept secret" to "booked solid"

I used the concept of the marketing starter to position myself when I was on the job hunt, and I used the three-phase approach to support that ideology. In conversations, I simply described what a marketing starter was and how I would fit into the role I was inquiring about. I clearly defined what I stood for and what my specialty was.

Your positioning statement should do the same. You see colleagues' positioning statements all the time—just take a look at their LinkedIn headlines or Instagram bios, and you'll see short and sweet highlights about who they are and what they stand for. Mine says "Marketing Starter" right in it, amongst other adjectives. A lot of people simply list their job title, but you can do better, because you're a marketer and you're not that boring. What would your marketing starter LinkedIn headline be, and how does it reflect your professional positioning?

## Be Prepared for Burnout

It's only when you're four Red Bulls deep into a day and spinning your wheels while longing for a sun-soaked beach vacation that you realize you might be teetering on the edge of burnout.

We should all be very wary of burnout. It happens to any over-worked professional, but even more so to starters who constantly build and hack their programs together. Even the greatest hustler will eventually run on fumes before they crash. And when they crash —not if—they crash hard. This is something that I would argue, just like an entrepreneur, a marketing starter is much more susceptible to than other marketers.

I have been on the edge of burnout many times—having a packed schedule of arduous, detail-demanding projects while trying to live life outside of work. I have always tried to keep it balanced, but when you have four huge projects that all culminate on the same day, there's not much you can do.

I came so close to a full burnout when my small marketing team was tasked with a brand and messaging refresh, creating a new website, launching a new marketing automation tool, and implementing a full CRM migration within my first six months on the job. Ah, those were the 12-hour days!

My team was burning out fast, but did we get the job done? Hell yeah, we did, but not without nearly breaking our backs. Each project, of course, had a bumpy landing when they were complete, which made our burnout diagnosis even worse.

It's not like they all had an abrupt end so we could finally kick back and coast for a minute. Since we pioneered so much with those megaprojects, there were bugs and fixes galore to be addressed. This comes with the territory of a marketing starter role and the company size—something I was prepared for.

> **TIP 46:**
> Always consider the possibility of burnout. Good time and expectation management is the only way to be prepared.

I did my due diligence during the interview process to understand the expectations of the role and the resources that were available to me. The last thing a marketer wants is to be surprised by potential burnout.

I became conscious of this in a job search where I had two competing offers on the table. One was for a smaller startup with the opportunity to completely build and shape their marketing department and lead a new team in charge of disruptive products, and the other was to lead a new team within a larger marketing team within a more established growth company that was quickly gaining market share.

Both had their plusses, both had their minuses. The startup would give me the opportunity to head all of the company's marketing and really make a huge impact if I put in long hours and birthed new creative tactics. The growth company would allow me to lead a smaller team but still be able to apply my skill set to a honed channel and sharpen my marketing acumen with learnings from upper marketing leadership. Both had great pay, company culture, and benefits, but what ultimately drove my decision was the burnout potential.

I was burnt out from a previous marketing starter role in which I was the sole marketing leader, and because the organization was smaller, I didn't have the opportunity to learn from or lean on more seasoned marketers above me. Sure, I was learning on the fly as I organized and built the marketing department under me (what a marketing starter often does), but that was my only learning pathway. That, on top of the stresses of a relatively flat leadership structure, added pressure to my role, which caused a lot of burnout. That sunny beach was sounding pretty nice during that time.

At the end of that job search, I ultimately chose the growth company role because it was a new position within a growing marketing department with two levels of leadership above me. It gave me the opportunity to learn from seasoned experts while also flexing my marketing starter muscles. I knew that the startup role would come with a lot of the same starter stresses as the previous one, and I wanted to lighten the load just a bit. At the risk of sounding like a sellout, I chose the role that I thought would balance my expertise, dedication, and ability to learn with the workload.

Some marketing starters may feel the same way and want to alternate their overwhelming workloads with ones that offer more work-life balance. Others may be just fine going from one hustle to another. Both are totally fine, because either way, you are able to apply your starter mentality. You just need to be conscious of the chance you may get completely burned out from starting over and over.

All I can say is, start wisely!

## There's No Room for Your Ego

Ladies and gentlemen, let me introduce you to the star of the show, our esteemed guest, the one and only... (insert your name here)!

It sure feels good to be the big shot, doesn't it? To be idolized for accolades and have your hard work put on a pedestal and your ego generously stroked. Heck, I know I love it! After all, it's only human to desire recognition for what you have accomplished. If you're someone who needs constant praise and ego-stroking, then you might meet a rude awakening when venturing into a marketing starter role.

I am going to warn you right now—because marketing starters are builders, creators, and strategic assemblers in the early phases of marketing projects—you may see a significant delay in recognition that might be well deserved. Granted, I have received my share of recognition during my marketing tenure, but it never came without the grind of the build beforehand.

Marketing starters need to check their ego and humble them-selves if they ever plan to make it off Marketing Island alive. Remember those sticky KPIs I talked about? Many of the ones marketing starters focus on may not be immediately tangible, which makes them hard to measure. This, in turn, may not make the starter next in line for a company-wide award for employee of the month.

I say to hell with that though! Marketing starters don't need a shiny glass obelisque to keep on their desk and collect dust. The satisfaction of building something cool is all marketing starters need to keep their momentum going. Giving up or failing to see a project through to the end? I don't think so. Starter OCD is what keeps them chugging away.

I am reminded of a meeting I once had with my marketing department's HR team lead. She set some time on my calendar about 90 days into my new gig to catch up and see how things were going. Thankfully, we left the office to grab coffee and have a casual chat. I was very pleased with the initiative to have a check-in like this. I had never worked for a company that found such interactions with new employees so valuable (take note HR starters out there!).

Anyway, during our chat, she asked how things were going so far in my role. Since she was part of my hiring process, she knew my role was created for me to fill and required a lot of starter mentality.

She asked if I was aware of my goals and asked about my experience working with my boss, the VP of corporate marketing.

What was most enlightening to both of us was when she asked about my experience working alongside my team. I described them as helpful and friendly, but because of the nature of my role, I was on my own to figure out what I needed to do. As a marketing starter, this is something I anticipated and was absolutely prepared for.

Nothing new to see here.

I described it as living on a little island of my very own, an island where I was the only inhabitant and I had to scrounge for supplies to eventually get off the island or make connections with the mainland nearby. I told her about my *Castaway* analogy—having to ration everything he found, build tools, hunt, and eventually make contact with civilization again.

Seriously, that analogy is a little gem for a marketing starter—at least you're part of a team who has resources at your disposal, and you have the ability to spin your chair around and greet your teammates on a daily basis.

Wilson!

Here's my point: Once you build bridges, or at least a boat, within your company or cast big smoke screens from your castaway beach, you'll get the recognition you deserve. Do you think we get some sort of award for making it off Marketing Island? I don't think so.

> **TIP 47:**
> It's hard to swallow your pride, but it's an important task for a marketing starter. Try your best not to get jealous, and put on a happy face when celebrating the successes of your co-workers while you're on Marketing Island. Your time will come.

I had to check my ego constantly in my marketing roles. I watched co-workers hire like crazy and build their teams. Many of them had chartered roles and open positions to fill, but not me! At least not right away. There was only one time that I was hired into a starter role where I had an immediate direct report and was able to quickly hire another.

Most of the time I have had to build my team from scratch following the growth of my programs. If having a team to manage is an ego stroke for you, check that right away. Sometimes having reports can hinder your agility as a starter. Of course, it's nice to have the help, but think about all the extra time and meetings you need to schedule just to properly manage them.

I promise one day you'll have a team and you'll get the recognition you deserve. Be prepared, though—sometimes your efforts may not bear fruit until long after you're gone. Or maybe you're the type that only likes to start and move on, and that's fine, too. You'll see other people take what you started and possibly turn it into something even greater than you could have imagined. That, my friend, would be the biggest ego check of all.

**Hey, False Starting Happens**

I've talked over and over about the marketing starter sweet spot: landing in a fast-growing company that is innovative, open, and in need of marketing pioneers. It truly is a "Goldilocks" situation where the porridge is just right. But honestly, there is a spectrum onto which marketing starters fit. Part of the marketing starter attitude is to be moldable and fit into the many different shapes and sizes that a business may require, even if it means coming into roles and situations that aren't so starter-minded.

I've been there about as many times as I have been in starter roles, and I have done my very best to apply my starter thinking while in them. But I have to admit, it is much more difficult to thrive in roles where "self-starter" isn't in the job description.

Part of the curse is this: you will inevitably find yourself in a role where your starter attitude is not well accepted and you might feel trapped. And that's okay. It's part of your learning experience as you decide where you want to be when you grow up in your career. These roles will certainly be a challenge to the starter-minded.

I remember doing contract work at a decent-sized medical staffing service company where I focused on rebranding initiatives. The gig was to re-write copy in the new brand voice and crank out as much as possible in the short three months I was there. But silly old me couldn't hold back my creative juices, and I quickly started coming up with new tones and positioning statements I thought would set the company apart.

Boy was I out of place. The manager to whom I reported got upset with me for not staying within my scope and made sure I understood that my job was to do their assigned tasks and nothing more. "Stay in your lane, kid!"

**TIP 48:**
Take a look at the job posting and get a feeling for how rigid the tasks are. Also, hop on LinkedIn to see whether the role is new or newly vacant. It never hurts to try to learn why the person who held that position left.

Shame on me for wanting to get creative and go the extra mile. Alas, it wasn't my place. Actually, I always want to broaden the scope of the project and get creative in short contract work. I mean, that's what marketing starters do! Of course, you can see the challenge here; roles with strict guidelines and little room for creativity might be hard for marketing starters.

Another pitfall to watch out for is finding yourself in a role that has been previously vacated by a marketer who has already built a thriving empire. I'm not saying that marketing starters can't meet the bar of whomever had the role before them or that we only like to do things our way. However, entering a role in which the previous marketer has already built successful programs would be a challenge to follow.

This is because the tactics are already proven, and any deviation (or creative switch-a-roo) could shake things up. Management may not be thrilled with fixing something that isn't broken. And even worse: It could lead to underperforming KPIs.

It's almost easier for marketing starters to thrive where nothing exists at all or where systems are significantly handicapped—again hinting at that sweet spot.

When something exists and is big, there is a higher likelihood that inefficient processes are in place, that people aren't pulling their weight, or that departmental reputational issues need to be overcome. All of these are things to consider during the interview process. There will always be a certain amount of false starts that you'll have to unravel in every role, but you need to decide what you are comfortable with.

My last little point is that you may not get to see your plans through. Rigid roles and roles that are already process-heavy are not ideal for starters like you and me, so you'll need to learn to let go of expectations that your grandiose plans will come to fruition while still fighting for what you believe in.

As professionals and, heck, as adults, we need to continuously reset our expectations. That's what I hope this book will help you do. The bottom line is this: It's easier for a marketing starter to thrive in a role that is new, because the lack of structure is where starters do their best work.

## There Will Always Be Risks

I'm not going to pretend for one second that there is no risk in becoming a marketing starter. In fact, the risk may be even greater than the more traditional, siloed approach to marketing. The broad strokes we take in pioneering our programs, combined with the types of companies and growth stages we choose, often create a cauldron of risk. I speak to that risk throughout this book and how to navigate it.

We should all mitigate these risks as much as possible, but there are certain ones that marketing starters should be keenly aware of. Starting something new may have a higher chance of getting cut or that it will fail.

**1. Getting cut** - If you haven't picked up on this risk already, then I don't know what to tell you, but getting cut is a huge risk to marketing starters. That cut could be in your department funding, program scope, or even your job itself— which has happened to me most frequently of all. Hopefully, you will find yourself at a company where you won't have to worry much about your job security, but you could always run into these other cuts. When cuts happen, it will certainly test your creativity, especially when it comes to your budget. Cuts are certainly something a starter can overcome. You'll just need to pad your budget and understand that it might happen.

**2. Lack of support** - Support is important to any role, but especially one in which you're starting from scratch and are already resource-strained. Even if everyone is on board with your role in the company and understands what you're there to do, there will be times when you simply won't have the support you counted on. This lack of support could come from upper management, your counterparts, or even your fellow marketers. This is where it's important for you to scream from the mountaintops what you need and why it's important for them to support you. No voice will be louder than your direct manager, so always make sure they're in your corner.

**3. Growth stagnation** - We're all sold on "hyper-growth" when we're interviewing, but stagnation can happen at any company at any time, even if they are the most funded data security tech company of all time! Projections are not always correct, and economic factors can play a significant part in growth slowing down. And when it does, your starter programs could feel it. When this happens, you need to decide if you want to wait out the delay or jump ship. Either way, do some serious investigation about what option suits you best.

**4. Stretching too thin** - This is honestly the most common risk to marketing starters and one you may certainly feel within the first month in your new role. With demands and requests coming at you from executives, customers, direct reports, and colleagues, it can seem overwhelming indeed. This is most prevalent in the marketing department of one. A few years ago, Angela Leavitt, founder of Mojenta Marketing based in San Diego, wrote a great blog post about how to survive being a marketing department of one. She really hits on what it's like to be a lone marketing ranger and shares some stellar tips to make it out alive. I highly suggest that you give it a read.

**5. Never getting it done** - I preach a lot about staying past the start so you can achieve real results with your programs and earn some accolades to show for it. However, there may be many times when that choice is taken out of your hands. This is one of the most frustrating risks, because I really like to see my systems in action. You may be this same way, but in the volatile world that marketing starters live in, we might have to move on before we get the chance.

# CHAPTER 12

## MARKETING METAMORPHOSIS

Only those who will risk going too far
can possibly find out how far one can go.

–T. S. Eliot
Poet

Turning to the Discovery Channel one day, the *Amazing World of Insects* caught my eye. Those little gross critters overwhelmingly dominate our planet in population and are wildly important to our fragile ecosystems. Their lives are so short but can seem even more complicated than ours at times.

Could you imagine living like a moth with two very distinct but equally important phases? One where you crawl and forage and then take a nap, and then one where you blossom and fly away? We've all heard that cliché, "you must crawl before you can walk," but I'll tell you that the moth takes it to a whole new level. They literally morph into a new version of themselves to take on the new challenges mother nature throws at them.

You, too, must morph when graduating from a marketing starter to a marketing grower. In chapter eleven, I encouraged you to stay beyond the start, to see your starter efforts through to the end, and even further. This is the fourth phase—the grower phase.

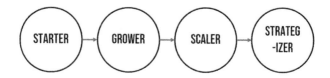

Being a marketing grower may not be for everybody. As with a startup founder, the excitement and the chase of the initial start, as well as the challenge of living on Marketing Island might be what excites you. But among the paths a startup founder might take, growth is certainly one of them. Now, marketing starters generally work for someone else's company, so this example is completely parallel, but the growth mentality can still be applied.

How many startup founders do you know who willingly jumped ship after they raised their series B and got their company into a hyper-growth phase? Imagine if Jeff Bezos left Amazon before the company crossed the 100-employee threshold? It's difficult to even picture that company without him (even now that he serves in the executive chair role). He and Amazon are one and the same! The other side of this coin is that many founders do eventually find their way to other endeavors after certain points of growth or acquisition, but the majority at least give it a shot.

In a company-wide meeting, Craig Walker, CEO of Dialpad, was once asked about his exit strategy and whether he was planning to sell or IPO in the near future. In response, he said, "A good company should never intend on selling." He went on to explain that he didn't build the company to sell it; rather, he built the company to grow it, employ amazing people, and create fantastic products.

At the time, Dialpad was nearing 500 employees and a $1 billion valuation. What would Dialpad have been like if Craig sold the company to a telecom mega-company before hiring employee number 100? He stayed beyond the start.

For those of you scared of the marketing-grower waters, or just not sure how to approach them, I have good news. You can still apply a starter mentality to marketing growing and get all the fancy

KPIs and pats on the back that you have been longing for as a marketing starter. Honestly, marketing growers need their own book, so stay tuned for that.

In my opinion, growth marketing as a whole actually comes easier than starter marketing. Marketing growers have more resources, more budget, and more headcount than starter marketers. They get more recognition too, but they are also more closely tied to tangible deliverables and metrics (i.e., lots of accountability there). They also might be a little more attractive to recruiters too, but they still need to keep starting close to their hearts.

Starters till the soil and plant the seeds, while growers apply fertilizer and water and then harvest the crop. It's up to you to decide which part you fancy most.

> **TIP 49:**
> Never hang up your starter hat! You can and should still apply your marketing starter tactics within your marketing grower role.

I see a few other phases beyond grower as shown in my chart above, including marketing scaler and marketing strategizer. However, all I'm going to say about those is that no matter the season of marketing you are in, you can always use the starter tricks up your sleeve.

# CHAPTER 13

---

## GET STARTED, NOW

Do not wait until the conditions are perfect to begin.
Beginning makes the conditions perfect.

–Allen Cohen
Author

Your marketing starter marathon is almost over! First off, thanks for taking the time to read this book and digest my sweet nuggets of wisdom. I hope you found the combination of starter mentality and marketing professional insightful and inspiring. I know I loved it when I first coined the idea; obviously, or I wouldn't have written this book about it.

The merriment of my two passions, entrepreneurship and marketing, has given me the unique ability to navigate the marketing world and work for some interesting companies. In an effort to put a bow on this, I want to leave you with a few final thoughts to consider as you continue your marketing journey.

### You're Human, Dummy

Obviously, you are human and it's impractical to assume you have the bandwidth to attempt all the suggestions and tips I provided in this book. In fact, it's in a starter's nature to have limited bandwidth, especially if you are a marketing department of one.

Unless you're some sort of superhuman being, you shouldn't dedicate a sizable portion of your energy to digging deep into any single one of these ideas—like reading every industry publication and competitor blog daily, for example. Before you know it, your day may be over and you didn't get anything done!

While starters are hustlers, at the end of the day we can only do so much before the rest of our systems suffer. My advice is to pick a few of these nuggets and find ways to apply them to what you do in the time you have.

And never forget, humans aren't perfect, so your marketing won't and shouldn't be either.

## What to Look for in a Company

As I mentioned at the beginning of the book, a marketing starter can exist within any company, but there are a few sweet spot scenarios I have found work best. Even if it's not a brand-new startup, it's more about the company's mentality or outlook on the specific role than the company itself. It doesn't matter the size, age, or what they sell. What matters is if the role is new and needs someone matching the starter metadata to build something new and exciting. That could be a startup's first marketing hire or a global legacy company looking to evolve in some interesting way.

In my personal experience, I have thrived mostly within small to mid-sized growth companies, ones that are agile and believe in the laboratory mindset and starting new things, but who also have a decent amount of internal resources to support my efforts. At the end of the day, the choice is yours, but you should carefully read the job description and ask the right questions about the role and team during the interview to get the preview you need.

**1. Traditional vs. exploratory culture** - I once read a job description for a VP of marketing that had "company-issued laptop" listed under benefits and perks. I immediately thought, "What kind of old-school company thinks that issuing a laptop is a benefit?!" That should be standard. Have you ever seen a job description say something like that? How about listing "paid holidays"? Why else would they list plainly obvious job features as benefits? Probably because they don't have any other benefits.

Now I'm just venting… but seriously, it's up to you to decide where you fit. Some like more traditional businesses, like, say, in the financial sector that are nine to five with 10 government paid holidays and 5-ft. x 5-ft. cubicles. Others like working from anywhere with free snacks, Red Bull (to help with the burnout), and unlimited vacation time. To each their own, but you need to decide. As I've said, a marketing starter role can be found in any company, in any sector, at any size—you just need to learn what to look for.

Companies that have a more exploratory and innovative culture will be more likely to hire a marketing starter. They are more willing to treat your programs like a laboratory rather than a factory and give you the wide berth you need to make them successful. They'll be more understanding of how it all works because they're figuring it out, too. Of course, you hope that they have some things figured out— enough that you can focus on marketing and hopefully not general operations. There's a fine balance you need to be okay with, but again, that's only for you.

While I was writing this section, a recruiter emailed me about an open position to gauge my interest. When he sent over the job description, I was absolutely ecstatic to see a company that had an exploratory culture and knew that they needed a starter to help them. Have a look at this example of a darn near perfect job description for a marketing starter. I bolded a few key items that jumped out at me.

Hi Tim,

I am reaching out about a full-time opening for a Director of Marketing with an exciting, rapidly growing B2B Logistics SaaS company, and I wanted to see if you'd be open for a conversation?

This would be the **first marketing role** within the organization, and you'd work alongside the Director of Sales and CEO to help take the company to the next level. This is truly a **blank canvas**, and this individual will have the opportunity to **create/build/influence** the marketing of the organization **from the ground up**. Currently, the company works with multiple outside agencies, and they're looking for this individual to **come in and take over** PR relations, demand gen, etc.

The ideal person will have an **entrepreneurial mindset**, come from a start-up environment, have proven success building a demand gen system, **someone who is hungry, who can roll up their sleeves, develop and run their show**.

In 12–18 months, this individual will have the opportunity to **move into a VP level** within the organization, and truly build a team from the ground up.

This opportunity allows for **high growth**, a chance to **build from scratch**, and the company is profitable and currently valued at $2 billion+.

Please let me know if you are interested,

Thanks

---

**2. Your manager's starter experience** - Has your potential new boss worked in a marketing starter role? Can they empathize with the journey you're looking to embark on? Boy, it sure would be helpful, wouldn't it? When you're on Marketing Island and taking the time to diligently start up your programs, you certainly will need an advocate, someone who will understand your approach and be able to defend you if needed.

Gather some questions to ask your would-be manager what their marketing journey has been like and how they plan to support your efforts. Remember the marketing starter curse? Your manager can really help you avoid many of the cumbersome pitfalls you may face.

**3. Small to mid-sized companies** - I mentioned at the beginning of this section that a marketing starter can live and thrive in any size company, but in my personal experience and professional observation, small- to mid-sized companies offer the best incubation places for marketing starters. Now, size definitions can be ambiguous and the term "startup" has been thrown around so much it has become completely commoditized, like how Kleenex has become synonymous with tissue or how "Coke" means any kind of fizzy drink in the south.

Sorry 1,000-person, 10-year-old tech company with series D funding and $50 million in revenue, you are NOT a startup. I know you're trying to keep a startup-minded culture, but you're not fooling anyone.

For the most part, every marketing role at a startup will be a marketing starter role, but mid-sized companies may offer the perfect intersection of starter mentality with support and security. Ultimately, you'll need to decide what size is best for you, but most of your opportunities will come from SMBs— at least that has been my experience.
It is almost like a spectrum. Brand new startups will have the most starter-oriented opportunities. Heck, even the office manager will be a starter! Mid-sized companies will have

plenty of starter opportunities, as well a little more structure to lean on.

And finally, large enterprises may have some solid starter roles, but unless they are launching something completely new, there will be a lot of current structure to navigate and bureaucratic tape to cut even in the most ideal starter role. My sweet spot has always been a small or mid-sized company, but it's more about the role and the attitude and mentality of the company rather than the size. I always keep an eye out for a newer, innovative company with seasoned and sharp executives.

You want enough structure to enable you to do what you need to do and execute your plans, but not so much structure that you feel your innovation and creativity are shackled.

**4. You want rapid growth, but not too rapid** - When you hear stats like, "We've grown 150 percent YoY" or notice on LinkedIn that they have grown headcount by 136% in the past 2 years, it can sound really attractive. Not going to lie, I have taken that bait many times, and you know my roller coaster story. However, there is merit to that old cliché: "Slow and steady wins the race."

Don't get me wrong, fast-growing companies can help accelerate your career and tend to be the best place for a marketing starter to call home. However, beware of fast-growing companies—especially if they are still looking for funding—because your starter course could potentially be very rocky. I'm not saying not to take a job with a fast-growing company, I'm just saying to be cautious. After all, we talked about riding the wave in chapter nine.

Fast-growing can often mean fast-bloating, and you don't want to be part of the bloat when they start making cuts to look better on paper. It's good to know how "rapid" the company is growing, whether they have laid employees off before, if they are revenue positive, if they are going to seek more funding, and if they are looking at acquisition.

Another important question is whether there is space and room for you to grow. As a starter, growth is what you make it, which means you can be as successful as you want to be—provided you put in the effort. This is why it's important to show that you know your craft and that you can create results and achieve success.

Room to grow also depends on the company itself. Even in a fast-growing company, you may find yourself not growing at all. Perhaps you aren't getting the support you were promised or the company's culture is not one that supports growth as much as you would hope. These are all good things to follow closely.

**5. Gauge the autonomy** - Your ability to roam free and get things done with your own expertise is paramount. You won't be able to survive with any level of micromanagement or overbearing oversight from executives. Honestly, this is probably one of the most important factors to consider when evaluating a potential company. You're going to need a ton of autonomy to both begin and maintain your programs. You should be abundantly clear when asking about how both the company and your prospective manager grant autonomy to their employees so you can set clear expectations for yourself.

I like to think of workplace autonomy as a sort of hierarchical structure with the company's core beliefs at the top. If the company doesn't believe in employing an autonomous workforce at the very top, then it most certainly won't trickle down to you. It all starts with trusting leadership.

Remember when I talked about the importance of trust? Well, you can't have autonomy without trust. Leadership needs to trust the professional adults they employ, and if you get a sniff at all that the company doesn't trust its employees, then that could be the smoking gun that autonomy has been shot dead.

Ultimately, though, the level of autonomy you will have will come directly from your supervisor. They will always have cultural and leadership influence in their mix, but they may be more willing to give you the open highway of autonomy than traditionally seen within the company, especially if they are marketing starters themselves.

During the interview process, ask your prospective manager if they will look to you as an expert and how they feel about autonomy within the role. One caveat is that the more junior you are, the less autonomy you will have, so keep that in mind. Don't expect to be able to do your own thing with your very first email marketing gig out of school. You have to earn it.

**6. Do you believe?** - Can you get behind the mission, the leadership, and the product? Do you understand what you sell and why you sell it (even though it doesn't matter what you sell)? Are you drinking the proverbial company Kool-Aid and sporting your branded hoodie everywhere you go?

Maybe you don't do all of that, but I hope you believe in the company if you're going to accept their offer of a job. At the end of the day, it should not be all about the money or your daily tasks. Hopefully, you can get behind what the company itself believes in—its why—so your heartstrings are tugged a bit when you roll up your sleeves and get started.

You should feel excited to talk about your company to your friends and colleagues alike. I joke about the hoodie, but I have a branded T-shirt from every company I have worked for in recent years. They make great workout shirts! If you can't find something to believe in at your company, it's probably time to move on.

**Are You Ready to Be a Starter?**

I can't say this enough: starting isn't for everyone and that's perfectly fine. The world is full of starters, growers, and everyone in between. If you are looking to venture out to build cool new things, then you took a good first step by reading this book. But like any good starter, sometimes you have to get a running start off the diving board and make a big splash with your cannonball.

There will always be another non-starter job if you ultimately decide you took the wrong path. But you might be ready if, after reading this book and talking with other marketing starters, you are excited and you think you have the organizational and self-motivational chops to see it through.

But really, it comes from inside. It's that internal drive that sets starters apart from their counterparts. That drive, combined with strong self-motivation, helps starters weather the storms of the rough marketing seas. Here are several questions you can ask yourself to check if you're ready to be a marketing starter:

**1. Are you self-motivated enough to make it off Marketing Island?** - I would be remiss if I didn't stress how important self-motivation is to marketing starters. Every successful entrepreneur you'll meet or read about overflows with self-motivation.

Just like them, marketing starters have the drive and persistent self-motivation to keep moving through their programs. Let's be real, this kind of marketing approach is not always the most glamorous. You may find yourself inundated with mundane tasks until you scale your programs and team so you can focus on what you really love to do. Keep your eyes on the prize to see it through. Pick up your favorite self-motivational book and take some notes to help you stay inspired!

**2. Can you balance daily tasks with your master plan?** - One of the most difficult things you'll have to do as a starter is learn to do daily and ongoing tasks while also building the foundation and framework for your programs. This is something uniquely acute to marketing starters because they have to build things from scratch with limited resources and limited human capital. It can be very straining to set time aside to craft a plan, then execute on that plan at the same time.

**3. Can you hone your communication skills on all levels?** - Did you go to school for marketing communications? Are you a master wordsmith or executive interpreter? Maybe you're not at the level today, but give it a few years and you might be.

As marketing starters tend to find themselves in mid-management roles more often than not, it is imperative to hone your interpersonal communication skills on all levels within a company. From account managers to support specialists, direct counterparts to the e-staff—you need to be prepared to speak the language and have empathy for anyone who intersects with your role.

**4. Are you able to advocate for yourself?** - This goes hand-in-hand with self-motivation, but you need to be your own sounding board. Don't expect others who are not in your marketing world to brag about you. You need to advocate for yourself. Be sure you are heard at company meetings and share the tangible fruits of your labor company-wide (when appropriate). Advocacy will make you less dispensable at the end of the day.

**5. Are you too afraid to fail?** - Fear can keep you safe when doing things like riding a motorcycle or free-climbing a cliffside, but it can be damn near paralyzing when attempting to start.
Starting relies on trial and error to figure out what path works best. Remember the lab vs. factory analogy from before? In a marketing lab, you might fail the first time you attempt to create something, and you can't be afraid to blow some stuff up in the process. If you're too afraid to make a mess, then you'll never learn from mistakes to create a better program.

Starters truly come in all shapes and sizes. The tactics you choose will vary greatly between marketing roles and whether or not you are in a management role. I'm not going to pretend that this book contains the magic formula on how to apply the starter mentality to every specific marketing role, but its content does serve up some ideas on how you can help yourself.

I think one of the saddest misconceptions about being a marketing starter is that we are dispensable, especially if what we're starting doesn't take off. It's always a good practice in a role to make yourself indispensable or un-fireable because you're the only person who has the domain expertise to keep your programs running. But when your programs aren't fully baked, it may appear you're more dismissable than others.

So I advise all the starters out there: Be huge self-advocates so you are seen as indispensable and a crucial part of the company.

And one final note for all the managers out there who currently employ marketing starters or plan to employ marketing starters. Please take this next point to heart. The starter mentality is special. The ability to combine the desire, tenacity, and skill to build something new while having the acumen to fuel success is rare. Hold on to your starters and never let them go. Give them all the room they need to spread their wings.

**TIP 50:**
Put down this book, roll up your sleeves, and get started!

# INDEX OF TIPS

**Tip 1:** Imagine your favorite marketing track (perhaps you're in it now) and ask yourself what you enjoy most about it. Think about what you would do if your boss asked you to scrap your current job description and rewrite the script of your role from scratch. Are you up to the task? This is a good thought experiment to see if you're a marketing starter.
Chapter 1, page 3

**Tip 2:** Create your own skills competency chart and see how you pan out. Be honest about your knowledge and skills to assess where you can grow and shape yourself into more of a T-shaped marketer.
Chapter 1, page 6

**Tip 3:** During your interview process, or when exploring a prospective role change, get an idea of what your Marketing Island looks like and what resources you'll have before you jump out of the plane.
Chapter 1, page 16

**Tip 4:** Ask your manager if they know the company's why. If they know, then ask how they apply that thinking to your team's duties. If they don't, then you should add this to your list of items to discover.
Chapter 2, page 21

**Tip 5:** Create a company-wide survey asking if your counterparts know the organization's *why*. Analyze the results to see how well aligned the organization is around the company's mission.
Chapter 2, page 22

**Tip 6:** Create daily Google Alerts for your company's name, your CEO, your industry, your customers, and key industry influencers to keep tabs on what's happening in your world.
Chapter 2, page 23

**Tip 7:** If you are in a marketing leadership role, attempt to become best friends with the sales leaders. Set up recurring meetings to help them advocate for marketing and vice versa.
Chapter 2, page 25

**Tip 8:** Schedule interviews with customer-focused representatives to get their perspective on the business. They have great intel on the customers' inner-most desires.
Chapter 2, page 27

**Tip 9:** Dig up all the customer marketing materials your company has created in the past. Read, watch, or listen to them—then talk to the content creators to learn more.
Chapter 2, page 30

**Tip 10:** Get through your basic business training, then ask for more. Set meetings with your peers and other managers to extend your training beyond what was assigned on day one.
Chapter 2, page 33

**Tip 11:** Find ways of interacting with the product or engineering teams to grasp the product; perhaps your company is hosting a training session you can attend. Or, you can set some time on the calendar for a deeper dive.
Chapter 2, page 35

**Tip 12:** Use your personal profiles to sign up for competitor newsletters and promos and follow them on social media. Also, visit their website to get served advertisements and watch their webinars to scrape their marketing tactics.

Chapter 2, page 37

**Tip 13:** To take inventory, create a spreadsheet of all marketing outputs. Then add columns for the statuses that work for you, like "freshness."
Chapter 3, page 40

**Tip 14:** Sketch a quick bubble map or flowchart to see how all the marketing tools work together in your company and what triggers them. Look for gaps and tweak the workflow in a way that works for you.
Chapter 3, page 42

**Tip 15:** Create a simple task sheet where you can see each team member's list of duties. This will help you better understand what they favor doing and how much of their time is spent doing it.
Chapter 3, page 43

**Tip 16**: Once your form or other simple marketing system is live, send a company-wide email (or to whomever your internal customers are) letting everyone know about the form's importance and process.
Chapter 3, page 47

**Tip 17:** Visibility and transparency are key. Whatever task manager you use, be sure your team and management can collaborate and see the workloads.
Chapter 3, page 48

**Tip 18:** Don't be afraid to fail or to sputter like an old motorcycle. Your systems will never be perfect in the first round. Be prepared to accept feedback and quickly iterate.
Chapter 3, page 50

**Tip 19:** Compile a list of quick wins and make time to complete

them in your first 30, 60, and 90 days. Including some that are cross-functional will always help to strengthen your plans.
Chapter 3, page 51

**Tip 20:** Lay out roles from the spectrum that are needed in your marketing department and describe how the roles inevitably morph over time.
Chapter 4, page 55

**Tip 21:** Create an online chat group for your marketing team or for specific projects, and make sure the chat is open on computers and phones during work hours so you can communicate easily with your team.
Chapter 4, page 57

**Tip 22:** Make your team feel as if there is as little hierarchy as possible to create a trusting environment. Always be willing to help out your team no matter how trivial the task and be a "get your hands dirty" kind of marketer.
Chapter 4, page 57

**Tip 23:** Jot down how you see yourself growing within your company and judge the feasibility before you start looking elsewhere. There may be a ton of opportunities right where you already are!
Chapter 4, page 59

**Tip 24:** Make your management style transparent. Don't surprise your reports; rather, set expectations early and give them tips for managing up to you.
Chapter 5, page 64

**Tip 25:** Create consistency and transparency within your team. Use documents and meetings to keep track and share what everyone is working on to create accountability.
Chapter 5, page 66

**Tip 26:** Make friends with the administrative assistants. They are the gatekeepers of the organization and can often help you out, especially if you're a department of one. Need a place to store your trade show booth? Your admin has the key to the closet. Need expo supplies shipped out on time? Well, guess who has access to the FedEx account.
Chapter 5, page 70

**Tip 27:** Patience is king when being the teacher. At times, teaching may be the most difficult part of your job. Hold meetings to delicately show your counterparts how to partner with you.
Chapter 5, page 71

**Tip 28:** Freemium is a lifesaver! Get as many free versions of tools as possible, and use the hell out of them until you absolutely need to spring for a paid subscription.
Chapter 6, page 78

**Tip 29:** If you're responsible for a budget, create a reverse balance sheet to track how much of your budget you use over time, so you know how best to allocate your funds as the year progresses.
Chapter 6, page 80

**Tip 30:** It is in your best interest to use all of your budget, but it's not always the best measurement tool to ask for more. Stay under budget if you can, and put some real metrics together to show your money at work.
Chapter 6, page 82

**Tip 31:** Don't be tempted by empire-building because it puts you at risk. Start small and make a clear growth path with the empire as a dream for later on. If you build too quickly, it can be stripped away just as fast as it was put up.
Chapter 7, page 85

**Tip 32:** When addressing a crisis, ask yourself these questions: What is the impact on the business? Is this really a crisis? Who thinks it's a crisis? What is your bandwidth to manage? What resources do you need to mitigate? The answers will help you judge how to tackle the issue.
Chapter 7, page 88

**Tip 33:** Budget 20 percent of your time/bandwidth for crisis management, last-minute projects, or other curveballs that might come your way, and use the rest on planned initiatives.
Chapter 7, page 89

**Tip 34:** Even though it doesn't matter what you sell, it's important to understand the product and how it's sold. Do your due diligence when you land the job at your new company and get up to speed on what they sell.
Chapter 7, page 93

**Tip 35**: Remove perfect from your vocabulary. Do it right now! A marketing starter has no room for perfect. We must churn and burn, build and measure. Always be striving for better, not perfect.
Chapter 7, page 97

**Tip 36:** As you're investigating your marketing infrastructure, learn how you can keep track of marketing ROMI with the tools you have at your disposal.
Chapter 8, page 100

**Tip 37:** People who pretend to know about marketing, or marketing posers, care a lot about vanity metrics. Be their guide and point them toward the right measurements.
Chapter 8, page 101

**Tip 38:** Compare your company's current list of marketing tools

against your wishlist, then request the ones you need to do your job the right way.
Chapter 8, page 102

**Tip 39:** Failure is scary, but you must embrace it. Sure, you may blow up the lab a few times, but think of all the ways you'll learn how *not* to blow it up in the future.
Chapter 9, page 106

**Tip 40:** Job security isn't real. Never assume that you're immune to layoffs or losing your job. This will keep you humble in your work and more composed when it happens. Ride the wave.
Chapter 9, page 110

**Tip 41:** In early sync-ups with your employees, ask them what processes and protocols would be dead in the water if they were to get hit by a bus. Then, have them write down how to operate them!
Chapter 10, page 112

**Tip 42:** Take advantage of your company's internal communication channels—whether it's an online chat room, internal emails, or company-wide meetings—to share your marketing wins. Take advantage of every opportunity to share how marketing is helping your team.
Chapter 10, page 113

**Tip 43:** Spreadsheets are your friend. Create spreadsheets with multiple tabs to track your budget, project metrics, and KPIs. Share it with your manager for easy access.
Chapter 10, page 115

**Tip 44:** Determine how you can apply tangible KPIs to your tasks. Write them down and track them over time. Those metrics will look great on your résumé.
Chapter 11, page 119

**Tip 45:** Develop your positioning statement. Keep it simple, relatable, and honest. It should reflect who you are professionally while offering a unique slant.
Chapter 11, page 122

**Tip 46:** Always consider the possibility of burnout. Good time and expectation management is the only way to be prepared.
Chapter 11, page 124

**Tip 47:** It's hard to swallow your pride, but it's an important task for a marketing starter. Try your best not to get jealous, and put on a happy face when celebrating the successes of your co-workers while you're on Marketing Island. Your time will come.
Chapter 11, page 127

**Tip 48:** Take a look at the job posting and get a feeling for how rigid the tasks are. Also, hop on LinkedIn to see whether the role is new or newly vacant. It never hurts to try to learn why the person who held that position left.
Chapter 11, page 129

**Tip 49:** Never hang up your starter hat! You can and should still apply your marketing starter tactics within your marketing grower role.
Chapter 12, page 135

**Tip 50:** Put down this book, roll up your sleeves, and get started!
Chapter 13, page 147

Download all these tips at
themarketingstarter.com.

# ABOUT THE AUTHOR

Tim Hines, a.k.a. "The Marketing Starter," is a marketing evangelist, keynote speaker, podcast show host, and author specializing in developing omni-channel programs for disruptive brands and cutting-edge tech. With almost two decades of experience, Tim has created strategic marketing initiatives with many industry-leading companies. He currently serves as Principal of The Marketing Starter Group, which specializes in getting marketing programs off the ground for rapidly growing businesses.

Connect with Tim at themarketingstarter.com, tnhines.com, on Twitter (@tnhines), and on LinkedIn (linkedin.com/in/tnhines).

Printed in Great Britain
by Amazon

78550568R00098